The collector's all-colour guide to

TOY
Trains

An international survey of trains and railway accessories, from 1880 to the present day

The collector's all-colour guide to

TOY

Trains

An international survey of trains and railway accessories, from 1880 to the present day

Ron McCrindell

TIGER BOOKS INTERNATIONAL
LONDON

A Salamander Book

This edition published in 1989 by
Tiger Books International PLC, London.

© Salamander Books Ltd 1985

ISBN 1 85501 025 9

Editor:
Richard O'Neill

Designer:
Barry Savage

Photography:
Terry Dilliway
© Salamander Books Ltd.

Filmset:
Modern Text Typesetting Ltd.

Colour reproduction:
Melbourne Graphics

Printed in Belgium.

Acknowledgements

We wish to thank the individuals and organisations listed below, without whose most
generous help this record of the toy trains of the 19th and 20th centuries could
not have been assembled.

All the trains and accessories shown in this book were made available from the
following collections:

Hadley Hobbies, London
Pages: 118-119 (part)

Allen Levy, The London Toy & Model Museum, October House,
21-23 Craven Hill, London W.2.
Pages: 40-41 (Collection of Ron McCrindell; on loan); 104-105; 106-107;
110-111; 114-115

Chris Littledale, The British Engineerium Museum, Hove, Sussex
Pages: 70-71; 72-73; 74-75; 76-77; 78-79; 80-81; 82-83; 84-85; 86-87; 88-89;
90-91; 92-93; 94-95; 98-99; 100-101; 102-103; 108-109; 112-113; 122-123; 124-125

Ron McCrindell, Sidmouth, Devon
Pages: 36-37; 38-39; 42-43; 44-45; 46-47; 48-49; 50-51; 52-53; 54-55; 56-57;
58-59; 60-61; 62-63; 64-65; 66-67; 68-69; 96-97; 116-117; 118-119 (part); 120-121

J. T. Van Reimsdijk
Pages: 22-23 (part)

Contents

Introduction

It is difficult to say with any certainty just when and how toy trains as we know them today first appeared. The earliest models appear to have originated in clock-making centres. According to Louis Hertz in his authoritative study "The Toy Collector", clockwork trains were first made in the United States of America by George W. Brown and Company of Forestville, Connecticut, in 1856; before that date, however, the clock makers of the German state of Bavaria (where Nuremburg was already a centre of the toy industry and would become the home of many great makers of toy railways) had already inspired several firms to produce primitive clockwork trains of the type that we now call "carpet toys" (because they were made to run not on rails, but on the floor).

In France, a model railway was constructed at St Cloud in 1859 for the Prince Imperial, the infant son of Emperor Napoleon III. This consisted of a figure-of-eight layout in approximately 8in (20cm) gauge, with a charcoal-fired steam locomotive that pulled three or four wagons. This was a grand and expensive toy to amuse the Imperial court; more practical, and of a still earlier date, were the model locomotives built for commercial demonstration and evaluation by many of the pioneer locomotive designers.

A number of the most distinguished British designers are known to have constructed such models, among them George Stephenson (1781-1848), designer with his son Robert (1803-1859) of the immortal "Rocket"; Richard Trevithick (1771-1833), who produced a model of his celebrated "Catch-Me-Who-Can" as early as 1797; and Timothy Hackworth (1786-1850), who produced a 4·25in (10·8cm) gauge working model as a preliminary to his "Sans Pareil" of 1826.

Following the famous Rainhill Trials, run on the Liverpool and Manchester Railway on 6-14 October 1829, when the Stephensons' "Rocket" established its superiority, and the subsequent opening of the Liverpool and Manchester as the first fully locomotive-operated public railway, the steam railway was firmly established and expansion of railway networks in most civilized countries was thereafter rapid. Great public interest was aroused, fortunes were made and often lost in wild speculation in railway construction, and, most significantly for our subject, small boys began to desire toy replicas of the "iron horses".

EARLY RAILWAY TOYS

The early toy trains were fairly crude representations of the real thing and were usually made of wood and unpowered, although for the better-off customer, expensive, hand-made, working models could be built to order. In any case, it was not until the 1850s that toy trains became generally

Below: *This figure is used to give an indication of scale on the photographic spreads. The Porter with Luggage Barrow is a hollow-cast figure made by Britains, Great Britain, in c1935; other examples of Britains figures are shown at (11-20), pages 120-121. Its height of 2·25in (54mm) makes it most suitable for use with a Gauge "1" layout.*

available. One of the earliest items to come to light, dating from that period, is an absolutely delightful toy called the "Rotary Railway Express". This consists of a tiny 2-2-2 locomotive and tender with two attractively-coloured carriages, all cast in lead and about 13in (33cm) long overall. The train is connected by a wire arm to a clockwork mechanism concealed within a decorative lead weight. Fortunately, this item was found, in a British antique shop, complete with its original wooden box, the instructions on which are well worth repeating:

"Having placed the weight containing the mechanism in the centre of a smooth table, attach the Engine to the weight by means of the wire, wind up the mechanism and the train will run a distance of about 150 feet (46m), to be considered the first station; detach one of the carriages and it will again proceed about 50 feet (15m), the second station; detach the other carriage and

the Engine and tender will run a considerable distance further making a total of nearly 300 feet (91m)."

The first commercial steam railway in Germany was the Ludwigsbahn, opened in December 1835, which ran between Nuremburg and Fürth. It is interesting to note that its first locomotive "Der Adler" (The Eagle) was built by Robert Stephenson and Company, thus reinforcing the fact that Great Britain was the true source of origin of the world's railways. (To celebrate the centenary of the opening of this line, Märklin produced in 1935 a magnificent Gauge "0" replica of "Der Adler" and its train, complete with driver and passengers: a one-off model made in limited numbers—and now extremely rare and expensive.) As has been mentioned, Nuremburg was already a toymaking centre when the line was opened—and very soon the local makers of lead and tin toys were producing for sale replicas of the new steam trains. At about the same time, toy trains, at first in lead and later in tinplate, began to appear in France, where the first public railway, from Saint-Etienne to Andrézieux, had been officially opened in 1828.

"PUSH-ALONGS" AND "PIDDLERS"

The early models were of simple "Rocket"-type locomotives, with carriages like those used on the Liverpool and Manchester Railway, in a design that owed much to the stagecoach (see illustration on *page 10*). Most models were roughly hand-painted and were unpowered "push-along" or "carpet toys". Simple clockwork models, like that described above, were later to appear, but in the earlier period most powered models were driven either by flywheel (the "friction drive" principle that has endured in mechanical toys up to the present day) or by steam.

The typical early steam-propelled, spirit-fired locomotives—popularly known to collectors now as "Piddlers" or "Dribblers" because of their tendency to leave behind them a trail of moisture from their cylinders—were usually of 2-2-0 or 2-2-2 wheel arrangement. The construction was almost invariably of brass, and oscillating cylinders were

Right: *Gauge "3½" "Stephenson's Rocket" Steam Train Set by Hornby, Great Britain, first produced in 1975 and still available. This large model bears no resemblance whatsoever to any previous train bearing the Hornby name; it was, in fact, made by Rovex Models of Margate, Great Britain, who acquired what was left of Hornby after the breakup of the Meccano company in the 1960s-70s. The locomotive is butane gas-fired and is fitted with piston-valve cylinders with oiler caps, and reversing gear; the boiler fittings include a water-filler cap, safety-valve, and a valve to prevent over-filling. Fuel is carried in the barrel on the tender, which is fitted with a control knob. The locomotive is marketed in its box (as shown here; for once the illustration on the lid matches the contents!), along with sufficient plastic track elements to make up a circle 8ft (2·44m) in diameter. The attractive "Liverpool and Manchester" Carriage (sold boxed, as shown, as a separate item) displays the strong influence of stage coach design on the railway cars of the 1820s-30s; indeed, it closely resembles three stage coaches joined together and mounted on a four-wheeled chassis. The "Rocket" should ideally be run out-of-doors; it can be run indoors by those with enough space—and for collectors and enthusiasts without the room to run it, it makes a pleasing display and conversation piece. It is modelled on the famous locomotive designed by George and Robert Stephenson, which was judged to be the best locomotive at the Rainhill Trials, run on the Liverpool and Manchester Railway (subsequently opened as the first fully locomotive-operated public railway) on 6-14 October 1829.*

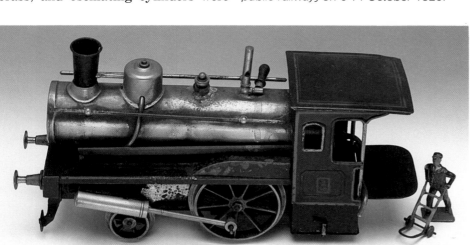

fitted. Such models were being made in Great Britain and France, where Paris was the centre of production, by the 1860s. In Britain, a major centre of production was the West End of London, where models were often made by optical and scientific instrument makers. Wood's of Oxford Street (founded by the father of Sir Henry Wood, the famous orchestral conductor and creator of the Promenade Concerts) was a prominent operator in this field as eary as 1860.

THE GERMAN MASTERS

On the European continent, toy trains in a form familiar to us today date from the later years of the 19th

Above: *Gauge "1" (note the gauge marked on the side of the cab) 2-2-0 Steam Locomotive by Carette, Nuremburg, Germany, dating from around 1895; an example of the type aptly nicknamed "Storklegs". These simple locomotives, fitted with twin oscillating cylinders, methylated spirit burner, safety valve, and, in the larger gauges, reversing gear, were initially marketed in Gauge "0" and "1", coming in a cardboard box with a circle of tinplate track. They were later available complete with tender and coaches, and in Gauges "2", "3", and "4". They had a long production run, still being catalogued, albeit in somewhat reduced form, as late as 1914. The origin of the nickname "Storklegs" for models of this kind is obscure: it is possibly of American origin and, as a look at the photograph will show, is obviously a fanciful allusion to the wheel arrangement. Length: 9in (22·86cm).*

century, with the establishment of great makers such as Gebrüder Bing (founded by the brothers Ignaz and Adolf Bing in 1863), Gebrüder Märklin (established under that name in 1880, at Göppingen), and George (*sic*) Carette (established in Nuremburg by the Frenchman Georges Carette, and at first with backing from Gebrüder Bing, in 1886). Also centring on Nuremburg were a number of lesser firms, some of whose products have now become as desirable for collectors as the toys of the most famous makers. Among these must be mentioned the names of Karl Bub (founded in 1851), Johann Distler (founded in the 1890s), Doll & Cie (founded 1898), Gebrüder

Fleischmann (founded in 1887, most famous for its toy ships, but still in operation as a maker of toy trains), S. Güntermann (founded before 1880), Hess (founded as early as 1826), Issmayer (founded 1861 and producing trains by the 1870s), Ernst Paul Lehmann (established in 1881 at Brandenburg-am-Havel), Ernst Planck (founded in 1886), and Jean Schoenner (founded in 1875).

A milestone in model railway development was set up by Gebrüder Märklin in 1891, when, at the Leipzig Spring Fair, the firm exhibited a clockwork railway set, with a figure-of-eight track, to which other elements could be added to expand the set. The wider importance of this Märklin "train set" is explained below under the heading "Gauges". Of equal importance to the development of model railways was the firm of Bing. Bing was in operation before Märklin: it first made toy trains in 1866, and would continue to do so until 1933, when a combination of increasing financial difficulties and the accession to power of the National Socialist regime of Adolf Hitler (the Bings being of Jewish extraction) forced the company to go out of business. In its heyday, Bing controlled an enormous factory in Nuremburg—in fact, the largest toy factory of all time, with some 5,000 employees before World War I—and manufactured not only trains but also a vast array of stationary steam engines, steam- and clockwork-propelled tinplate ships and automobiles, electric-powered toys, magic lanterns and slides, and, as early as 1902, cinematographs and films, together with a huge range of toy railway accessories and all kinds of novelty toys.

The third of the "big three" German makers was Georges Carette. His company remained in production only until World War I, when the French-owned, Nuremburg-based firm was forced to go out of business in 1917. Märklin is the only one of the three to remain in production today, with toy trains in "Z", "N", and "00" Gauges, and an impressive variety of Gauge "1" items (all now electrically-propelled, and mostly of plastic construction).

BASSETT-LOWKE OF BRITAIN

However, in spite of the great activity in Germany before the turn of the century, the man who is, in the present author's opinion, best-entitled to be called "The Father of Model Railways"—certainly of model railways as we know them today—is Wenman J. Bassett-Lowke of Great Britain. Having been brought up in a family firm that built and maintained steam machinery for the footwear industry of Northampton, Bassett-Lowke founded a company to make castings for build-it-yourself model locomotive enthusiasts in 1899. While visiting the Paris Exhibition of 1900, Bassett-Lowke was most impressed by the products of Märklin, Bing and Carette. The products of the two latter firms were later to form an important part of his catalogue of items for sale in Great Britain.

However, his initial commercial contact was with Bing, since he observed that some Bing locomotives would, with slight modification, pass very well as representations of British prototypes. He was also impressed by Bing's steam mechanisms, with piston-valve, double-acting cylinders. Thus began an association between Bing and Bassett-Lowke that lasted until the German factory closed its doors in 1933. The many fine British-style trains supplied over the years by Bing for marketing in Great Britain by Bassett-Lowke now rank among the most desirable collector's items—and many are shown on the photographic pages of this book.

GAUGES

At this point, where we enter the period of the "modern" toy railway, and where mention of "gauges" will become increasingly frequent, it is desirable to give a fairly full account of the origin and meaning of this system. "Gauge" may be defined as the distance between the centres of the rails; and up to about 1890 there were no standardized gauges for model railways. The brazen "piddlers" and "dribblers" of the 19th century were built in a multiplicity of sizes by a number of different makers, all of whom were concerned only with their own products and paid no attention at all to the proportions of trains produced by other makers. It therefore devolved upon the early commercial makers of tinplate toy trains to attempt to bring order to this chaos.

As has already been mentioned, Gebrüder Märklin exhibited a clockwork train at the Leipzig Spring Fair of

1. *Gauge "2½" (in fact, Gauge "3"; but more correctly described as "2½" in the case of this fine model) 4-4-0 North Eastern Railway (NER) Locomotive, numbered "1619", and Six-Wheeled Tender, made by Carette, Nuremburg, Germany; a very rare item, first catalogued in 1905 and available in Great Britain from both Bassett-Lowke and Gamage's. The latter priced it at £5 5s 0d (£5.25, $6.30), just undercutting Bassett-Lowke and thus setting the tone of the retail rivalry that existed between the two firms. In spirit-fired steam, the locomotive is unusual for its time in being fitted with high-pressure cylinders, Smithies-type boiler, and link reversing operated from the cab. The example shown here has been restored. At first, no carriages were available to run with this locomotive, but in 1909 Carette issued beautiful Gauge "2½" bogie coaches in crimson NER livery: see photograph on page 18. Length (engine and tender): 27in (68·58cm).*

2. *Gauge "2" 4-4-0 "County of Devon" electric Locomotive, numbered "3835", and Six-Wheeled Tender, in the correct Great Western Railway (GWR) livery. This model was marketed in the UK by Bassett-Lowke in 1912 but, unlike the majority of the Bassett-Lowke items shown in this book, it is neither German-made, nor of tinplate. It was, in fact, made by one of several British firms that were supplying models to Bassett-Lowke at around that time. It is fitted with Bassett-Lowke's early electric motor, the "Universal Lowko" motor with "Patent Automatic Reversing Switch", working on 8-12 volts. A massive and weighty model, it is constructed of mild steel plate and sheet brass, with turned cast-iron wheels. Originally selling for around £10 0s 0d (£10.00, $12.00), it is now fairly rare, and is a most pleasing model, with detail that includes a coal top on the tender. However, models like this are not as eagerly sought by collectors as their German-made counterparts. Length (engine and tender): 26in (66·04cm).*

3. *Gauge "1" 4-6-0 "Sir Gilbert Claughton" steam Locomotive and Six-Wheeled Tender, in London, Midland & Scottish Railway (LMS) livery and numbered "5900". The prototype, named after the chairman of the London and North-Western Railway (L&NWR), appeared in 1913, and Bassett-Lowke had the model catalogued in Britain by 1914. The initial models, in the correct L&NWR black livery, were made by Bing, Germany, but the example shown here is from a small batch assembled at Northampton and marketed by Bassett-Lowke at the end of World War II. They can be distinguished from the earlier models by the smaller bosses on the driving wheels. Only about 400 of these model locomotives were produced, in Gauge "1" steam only, and they are not easy for collectors to find. Length (engine and tender): 25in (63·5cm).*

4. *Gauge "0" 4-4-0 "George the Fifth" clockwork Locomotive and Six-Wheeled Tender, numbered "5320", made by Gebrüder Bing, Nuremburg, Germany, for sale in Great Britain by Bassett-Lowke. This example dates from the mid-1920s, but the model was available as early as 1912 and was made in large numbers until well into the 1920s. It was originally available—as shown at (7-8) on pages 54-55—in the true-to-prototype black livery of the London and North-Western Railway (L&NWR), numbered "2663", but subsequently appeared in several different liveries—it is shown here in London, Midland & Scottish Railway (LMS) colours—and with different names, including "Minerva" and "Queen Mary". It was made in Gauges "0", as shown, "1" and "2": it was available only in black in the two larger gauges, and a "de luxe" model, with generally superior finish and better-scale wheels, was available in Gauge "0". It was made in both clockwork, as seen here, and electric versions and, because of its long production life, is not too difficult for the collector to find in one or other of the various versions produced. Length: 16in (40·64cm).*

1891. The figure-of-eight track on which this model ran was 1·89in (48mm) wide. Whether or not that was the first train made by Märklin in that gauge is not at all certain; but what is certain is that very shortly afterwards Märklin was cataloguing the 1·89in (48mm) size as Gauge "1", along with 2·125in (54mm) as Gauge "2", 2·95in (75mm) as Gauge "3", and, for the very smallest trains then produced by the firm, 1·38in (35mm) as Gauge "0". (Roman numerals were then used to express gauges by Märklin and other makers; however, to avoid any confusion, the conventional figures more often seen today are used throughout this book.)

These early Märklin clockwork trains, described in the firm's catalogue as "Eisenbahnen mit Uhrwerk auf Schienen" ("train with clockwork on rails"), were of the type now popularly known, from their very large driving wheels, as "Storklegs" (see page 8), but with 0-2-2 wheel arrangement rather than 2-2-0 configuration. They were supplied as a set, along with two or three four-wheeled carriages and an oval of tinplate track—or, at a slight

extra cost, a figure-of-eight track. Both forms of track layout subsequently became very popular: the oval, in particular, featured as an essential part of almost every train set made.

Such features as points and turntables were soon added to Märklin layouts, together with a wide array of accessories, ranging from elaborate and beautifully hand-painted stations, railway buildings of all kinds, and tunnels, to signals, level crossings (grade crossings), bridges, and—to add realism to the train itself—the terracotta figures of passengers, to be horrendously impaled on the metal spikes fitted to the seats of the little carriages.

By 1894, Märklin's great Nuremburg-based rival, Bing, was offering very similar trains and recommending them, in its catalogue, as suitable for children up to ten years old. Bing offered its trains in gauges of 1·46in (37mm), approximating to Gauge "0"; 1·89in (48mm), the same as Märklin's Gauge "1"; and 2·36in (60mm). From these figures it will be seen that although, at this early time, Bing's gauges were not standardized with

1

2

3

4

Left: *Tinplate Railway Station by Gebrüder Märklin, Germany, dating from 1900 or possibly earlier: it was catalogued in Great Britain by Gamage's, London, in 1902 — described as an "enamelled railway station . . . beautifully finished" (as indeed it is!), and priced at 12s 6d (62½p, 75c). A superb, gorgeously hand-painted item, this is rare — and extremely rare in this virtually mint and complete state. The station is in continental style: a French version is shown, and it was also produced with English, German, or Italian lettering. It was presumably intended for use with railways of any gauge; however, the Gauge "3" railway official standing at the archway (note the barrier and the ticket-office counter just visible in the passage behind him) appears to be about the right size: compare the figure to our "Scaleman" of approximately Gauge "1" dimensions. Base: 13·75in x 8·75in (34·925cm x 22·225cm); maximum height: 11·75in (29·845cm).*

those of Märklin, they were at least approaching that state. In 1895, however, Bing issued a catalogue listing steam locomotives and rolling stock in gauges of 1·38in (35mm), 1·89in (48mm), 2·125in (54mm), 2·64in (67mm), and 2·95in (75mm); respectively, Gauges "0", "1", "2", "3", and "4", as they were to become known. (It should be noted that at this time Bing's clockwork trains were offered in Gauges "1" and "2" only.)

Following the lead originally given by Märklin and taken up by Bing, the other German makers, including Carette, Bub, and Planck, adopted the same track widths for their products, and thus the gauges of toy trains became standardized.

Above: *Early toy railway accessories in tinplate. (Left): Tunnel, used by the owner on a Gauge "1" layout but capable of accommodating trains up to Gauge "3", made by Gebrüder Märklin, Germany, around 1900. This attractive, hand-painted tinplate tunnel incorporates public viewing galleries and pleasingly detailed landscape features. The present author, on whose layout it is now a feature, has improved on those details by adding "fir trees" that were probably originally intended as decorations for a Christmas cake: they are, it must be admitted, quite convincing! (Background, left): Tinplate Signal by Gebrüder Bing, Nuremburg, Germany, again dating from around 1900 and intended for use with any gauge (although best-suited to larger gauges). The lever protruding from its base can be set between tinplate rails to engage the automatic brake of a clockwork locomotive, thus stopping the train with the signal at "Danger". (Background, centre): Clock and Indicator, an early tinplate accessory, probably made by Bing. (Background, right): Platform Crane; a nice example of an early hand-painted tinplate accessory by Bing, with the simulated brickwork typical of Bing at that period. (Foreground, right): Double Turnstile by Carette, Nuremburg, Germany, again dating from around the turn of the century; a particularly charming item, beautifully hand-painted and complete with the terracotta figure of a ticket collector wearing a blue uniform.*

AMERICAN PIONEERS

In the United States of America, as in Europe, the first toy trains worthy of note were steam-driven models. One of the most notable among the earlier makers was Eugene Beggs of Paterson, New Jersey, a former fireman on the Mariette and Cincinatti Railroad, who obtained a patent for a model steam locomotive in 1875, Beggs' model was of approximately Gauge "1" proportions and had a 4-4-0 wheel arrangement, with an appearance much like a tank engine. Its wheels were set to run in a circle, and track made up of steel strips set into wooden sleepers was supplied. Of particular interest were the bogie cars made to run with the locomotive: these had cardboard bodies covered with brightly lithographed paper. Because of their fragile construction, very few of these have survived, and they are now greatly prized by American collectors. Beggs' steam trains remained in production until the year 1906.

Also active in the United States at this earlier period was the mechanic and inventor William Weeden of

Right: *Gauge "2" London and South-Western Railway Train by Gebrüder Bing, Nuremburg, Germany, shown as catalogued in Great Britain by Bassett-Lowke in 1903: a most attractive and rare item. It is beautifully hand-painted, the apple-green livery of the clockwork 4-4-0 locomotive, numbered "593", and six-wheeled tender, being complemented by the charming pink, brown, and white of the carriages. It was offered in the livery shown — in the author's opinion, the most attractive — and in the colours of the Great Northern, Midland, and London and North-Western Railways. It was available in Gauges "0", "1", and "2", and in clockwork or steam. It is worth noting that demand for Gauge "2" models, popular in the early years of the century, had virtually ceased by the time of World War I; in fact, in the early 1920s Bassett-Lowke actually fitted some Gauge "2" models with Gauge "1" wheels and catalogued and sold them as Gauge "1" items. Lengths (engine and tender): 19·5in (49·53cm); (passenger coach, third class): 13·5in (34·29cm); (brake van): 10·5in (26·67cm).*

Inset: *(Left) Gauge "0" Snow Plough by Jean Schoenner, Nuremburg, Germany; a most interesting and unusual model from a maker who appears to have ended production around 1906. It is of soldered construction, with detail pressings that include rivets, and is hand-painted. It is doubtful if the needle-sharp point of the plough blade would be permitted in a toyshop subject to modern safety regulations! Length: 6·5in (16·51cm). (Right) An 0-6-0 Carpet Toy Locomotive by Rossignol, Paris, France. This attractive floor train, in no particular gauge and with unflanged wheels, dates from around the turn of the century and, for a simple toy, is a fairly reasonable representation of a locomotive of the period. It is clockwork-powered (note the fixed key). It displays some very interesting bright early lithography, and its boiler bears the legends "France", "CR", and "6000", all in rectangular panels. Such floor trains sometimes had axles angled so that they would run in a circle. The collector should note that most lithographed toys like this were made of thin-gauge tinplate: corrosion may occur because of the relative thin-ness of the finish. It is of considerable interest to compare this fairly early floor locomotive with the Japanese-made toys of the same kind shown in the photograph on page 36. It will be seen that both the Rossignol train and the friction-powered toys made some sixty years later rely mainly on bright lithography for their appeal. Length: 8·25in (20·955cm).*

Massachusetts, who established the Weeden Manufacturing Company in 1882. At the request of the editor of "The Youth's Companion" (a juvenile publication; the US equivalent of the celebrated "Boy's Own Paper" of Great Britain), Weeden designed and built in 1888, as a competition prize for the journal, the "Weeden Dart". This was a simple spirit-fired 2-2-0 locomotive, of approximately Gauge "2" proportions, with oscillating cylinders and fitted with a non-operating headlight and a pilot (the latter feature is that popularly known, although the term is not favoured by American railway enthusiasts, as a "cowcatcher"). Later a tender and lightweight bogie cars were

made available to run with the locomotive on track similar to that made by Beggs. Some 10,000 examples of the "Weeden Dart" are believed to have been made and sold at the modest price of £2.08 ($2.50).

Weeden continued to produce steam-propelled trains, boats, vehicles, and some electric toys, until his death in 1889. His company, under William Ritschie, continued to produce trains until 1910 and, in the 1930s, resumed production in the field with an electrically-fired steam locomotive in Gauge "0", which, however, made little impact.

Another American maker of note active in the 19th century was John Garlick, who had worked with Beggs

and whose steam locomotives much resembled those of his former employer. Garlick, who is also known to have experimented with electric-powered models, was active in Paterson, New Jersey, until around 1904.

EUROPEAN EXPORTS

By that time, from the turn of the century, the products of such German makers as Bing, Märklin, Carette, and Schoenner had begun to appear on the American market. Some of their models, notably the large and highly decorative examples by Schoenner, were "floor trains" (ie, like "carpet toys", not meant to run on rails) and were of correct American appearance

in outline and livery). Others, including many of those made by Bing and Märklin for running on rails, were European-style locomotives to which such typically American features as pilots and bells were added. In either case, these models exported from Europe were generally far superior to the toy trains being made in the United States at that time.

(It may be noted here that Märklin, in spite of its early cavalier attitude, was later to produce some very fine trains in authentic American outlines, powered by steam, clockwork or electric, and usually in Gauges "0" and "1". Notable models, dating of course from a much later period than that

discussed above, were the magnificent "New York Central" Hudson-type 4-6-4 locomotive, in Gauge "0" electric, and a superb version of the streamlined "Commodore Vanderbilt".)

To return to the early 20th century: Carette scored a great success in the United States in 1904 with its splendid "New York Central" Vauclain Compound 4-4-0 Express locomotive, made in Gauges "1" and "2" and in both steam and clockwork. As well as being exported to the USA, this model was marketed in Great Britain by Bassett-Lowke: it is now extremely rare, and a highly desirable collector's item which is eagerly sought after on both sides of the Atlantic.

ELECTRIC POWER

As I have already stated, the first toy trains to run under their own power were steam-driven, and these were soon followed by friction- and clock-work-propelled models. Electric-powered models were, however, earlier on the scene than is, perhaps, generally supposed. Ernst Planck, a Nuremburg-based firm that produced magic lanterns and stationary steam engines from 1866 onward, advertised an "Electric Railway and Electric Motors" for sale as early as 1880. However, although Planck exhibited an electric railway that aroused great interest at the Bavarian Trades Exhibition of 1882, little is known of these early models

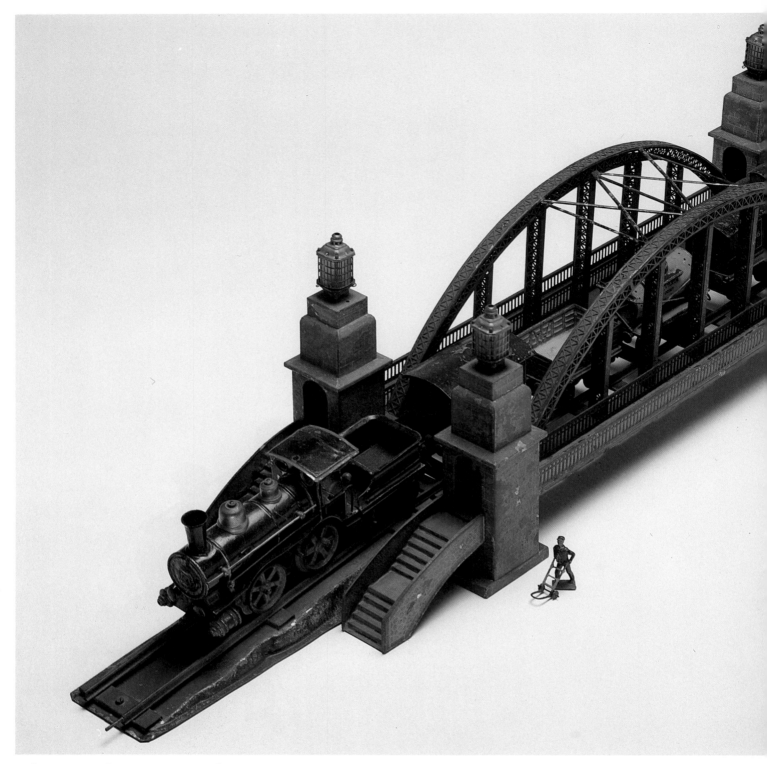

and no examples seem yet to have come to light. Planck remained in production with simple steam, and later clockwork, locomotives, as well as other toys, until the 1930s.

In the United States, too, electric toy trains appeared at a quite early date. They were quick to gain popularity in the USA, perhaps more so than in Europe; possibly because electrically-driven passenger railways were in service in the USA, from the 1890s onward, at a generally earlier date than elsewhere. In the early 1880s, the Novelty Electric Company of Philadelphia advertised a toy "locomotive driven by electricity". Another pioneer in this field was the Voltamp Electric

Manufacturing Company of Baltimore, Maryland, set up by Manes E. Fuld, who designed an electric railway as a Christmas present for his son in 1879. From around the turn of the century, Voltamp (in operation under that name until 1923) produced a wide range of locomotives, all electric-powered and in both electric and steam outlines, with rolling stock (including imported items made by Märklin), to run on 2in (51mm) gauge steel-strip track. The models operated either off a 6-volt wet battery, or by "street current"; ie, from mains electricity, with the aid of a transformer—a device that Voltamp was the first to introduce.

In Great Britain, in 1903, Bassett-

Lowke advertised for sale an "Electric Tramway", made in Gauge "1" by Carette, to run off "two bi-chromate glass cell batteries". At the same time, Bassett-Lowke's Catalogue listed "Central London Railway" four-wheel locomotives of the "steeple cab" type. These were made by both Bing and Märklin, and were available in clockwork as well as electric. Electrically-propelled trains in steam outline were very soon added to the Bassett-Lowke Catalogue, and it became general practise to offer new items in a choice of steam, clockwork, or electric. Although emphasis had, within a few years, veered to clockwork and electric at the expense of steam, a fair number

Left: *Gauge "1" Railway Bridge by Gebrüder Märklin, Göppingen, Germany, dating from around 1910; one of the most impressive of Märklin's beautiful bridges and, with a length of 57in (144 78cm), one of the largest made. Apart from some paint loss, this example is in superb condition and is complete with its four working oil-lamps, one at each corner. It is extremely rare and valuable, for early toys of this size and complexity are all too often found in damaged condition or with parts missing. The bridge is a study in true model engineering, featuring the ingenious use of pressed parts from certain other Märklin structures and presenting a most realistic appearance. The train shown on the bridge is a typical item dating from around the turn of the century: the four-wheeled locomotive with its tender, and the van, open wagon, oil tank wagon and guards van are all simple tinplate railway items produced by Gebrüder Märklin.*

Above: *Gauge "0" Single-Track Engine Shed by Gebrüder Bing, Nuremburg, Germany, dating from 1900. This pleasing hand-painted and -enamelled accessory was available also in larger gauges and with twin tracks. It appears to have remained in production until World War I, and was advertised for sale in Great Britain by A.W. Gamage, London, in 1913, with three-rail electric twin-track, at a price of 10s 6d (52½p, 63c). Length: 11in (27·94cm); maximum height: 6·25in (15·875cm). The engine seen in the doorway of the shed in this photograph is an early Bing steam locomotive, dating from around 1895. Note the monogram trademark "GBN" (for "Gebrüder Bing, Nuremburg") clearly visible on the front of the locomotive in this photograph. It is interesting to compare this engine shed with the later Gauge "0" E2E Engine Shed by Hornby, Great Britain, produced in the 1920s and 1930s which is shown on page 19.*

of steam models continued to be available and a number of fine new steam trains were added to the Bassett-Lowke Catalogue.

HORNBY TRAINS

Despite the pre-eminence of Bassett-Lowke, with its German-made trains, in the earlier period in Great Britain, the most famous of all British-made toy trains—both in Britain itself and on the European continent—were those of Hornby. So wellknown were they that, in the 1920s and 1930s, it was not uncommon to hear any tinplate toy train, whatever its origin, described as "a Hornby" (rather as all household vacuum cleaners tend to be

referred to as "Hoovers"!).

The Liverpool-born Frank Hornby (1863-1936) had, in 1901, obtained a British patent for the invention he called "Mechanics Made Easy": this was the famous "Meccano" construction system of metal strips with perforations for nut-and-bolt assembly, and the Meccano trade-name was adopted a few years later. However, surprising though it may seem, the date of the first appearance of Hornby trains cannot be stated with any certainty. Some respectable authorities hold that Hornby trains were available before 1914, or that they first appeared in limited numbers, in Gauge "0" clockwork, in 1915 and were available during

World War I, but these assertions have never been satisfactorily verified. However, it can be stated that Hornby clockwork trains were certainly being catalogued by 1920, under the name "Hornby Trains"; electric-powered Hornby trains first appeared in Britain around 1925.

EARLY HORNBY MODELS

The first Hornby trains came in bolted-together form; they owed many design characteristics to Meccano and were, in fact, assembled with Meccano nuts and bolts. The first Hornby train set consisted of a small Gauge "0" 0-4-0 clockwork locomotive, numbered "2710", with a tender and an open

wagon. Available in black, green, red, or blue (blue examples are now very rare), it came with an oval of tinplate track, and the set was marketed in a cardboard box with simulated leather finish. A singular feature was the fitting of buffers and couplings between engine and tender, as Bing had done in the 1890s. A 4-4-0 locomotive and tender soon appeared (quickly followed by a 4-4-4 tank locomotive), and in this model the buffers between engine and tender were omitted.

Hornby trains quickly became very popular, and the Hornby trademark appeared until World War II on a comprehensive range of toy trains that were familiar items in almost every

British household where there were children.

The Hornby Dublo (ie, "Double 0", Gauge "00") range of trains—illustrated in this book on *pages 112-113*—made in both clockwork and electric, first made its appearance in 1938. At about the same time, Hornby set a higher standard of truth-to-prototype with a relatively accurate Gauge "0" model of the Southern Railway "Schools Class" locomotive "Eton"; see (5) on *pages 92-93*. This was shortly followed by Hornby's most celebrated model, "Princess Elizabeth",issued to coincide with its prototype, which had just made a record-breaking run on the London, Midland & Scottish Railway

(LMS) line between Euston Station, London, and Glasgow, Scotland.

The well-proportioned and finely-detailed model of the famous LMS Pacific (ie, with 4-6-2 wheel arrangement) was available in electric only and was sold in a special presentation box at a cost of £5 5s 0d (£5.25, $6.30)—a high price for a Hornby locomotive. Although Hornby's contemporary catalogue stated that, for the benefit of those purchasers who already had complex and expensive layouts, "Princess Elizabeth" was capable of being run on the 2ft (0·61m) radius tinplate track available up to that time, the locomotive could not, in fact, give its best performance on that

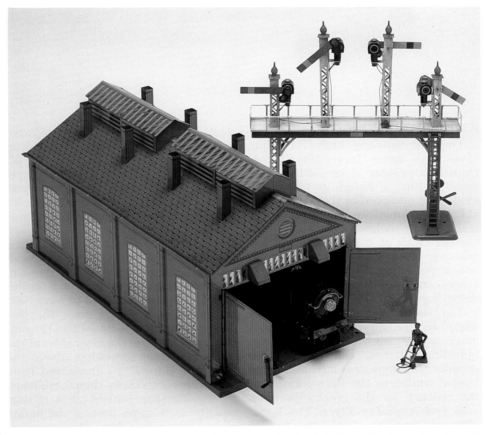

Left: *Gauge "2½" (Gauge "3") 4-4-0 North Eastern Railway (NER) Locomotive, numbered "1619", and Six-Wheeled Tender, made by Carette, Nuremburg, Germany (and fully described on page 10), shown here with a pair of coaches brought out by Carette to complement it in 1909. Finely lithographed in the crimson livery of the NER—they were also available in L&NWR colours—the Passenger Coach (right) follows the usual Carette pattern of division into five compartments and two lavatories, and has opening doors (which were not generally fitted to smaller-gauge items). The Full Brake Van (left) has two pairs of opening baggage doors on either side and is provided with a guard's (conductor's) look-out. Both coaches are fitted with turned cast-iron wheels, another refinement generally found only on larger-gauge items. Length (each coach): 20·5in (52·07cm).*

Below: *Gauge "0" E2E Engine Shed by Hornby, Great Britain, fitted for electric track and with electric lighting. This model had a long production life, appearing in the late 1920s and continuing until World War II; it*

was also available in the No 2 clockwork version. The nicely-detailed building features roof lights and chimneys, guttering, and opening doors. It was quite highly priced, selling at around 15s 0d (75p, 90c) in the 1930s. Note that the catalogue numbers of Hornby's electric items had the prefix "E", and sometimes both prefix and suffix "E", as in this case, to indicate both electric track and electric lighting. This model is popular with collectors, and examples with bright lithography are eagerly sought after. Length 19·5in (49·53cm); maximum height: 10·25in (26·035cm). With it is a Gauge "0" No 2E Signal Gantry by Hornby; an over-scale but attractive item available from the late 1920s until World War II. The example shown is in excellent condition, although such models are obviously among the most vulnerable of model railway structures. The example shown here has survived intact because it remained in its original box. The No 2E version is electrically-lit; it was also available without electric lighting, as the No 2 Signal Gantry. Height: 13·5in (34·29cm).

track, so steel track of superior quality and of 3ft (0·914m) radius was made to go with the model. Both locomotive and track were made over a comparatively short period of time and both are now rare: all Hornby train production ceased in 1940, and very few items from the pre-World War II Hornby series reappeared when the firm went back into production in 1946.

IVES OF CONNECTICUT

One of America's leading makers of the 20th century emerged as the result of what at first seemed a serious setback to any commercial success. Edward Ryley Ives of Bridgeport, Connecticut, had been active as a

maker of tinplate toys, including clockwork "floor trains", since the early 1870s, although from the 1880s he had produced only cast-iron floor trains. In the 1890s, Ives' firm was in serious financial difficulties, and in December 1900 Ives suffered the loss of all his tools and equipment in a fire. He was forced to start afresh—and this proved to be a blessing in disguise: influenced and inspired by the products of the Nuremburg makers, especially Märklin, who were putting indigenous makers under increasingly heavy commercial pressure, Ives invested in new machinery with which, from 1901, he began to produce simple clockwork trains in Gauge "0", which were

supplied with Märklin-type track and were compatible with the products of the German toymakers.

Gauge "1" trains appeared from Ives in 1904. The overall characteristic of Ives' earlier trains was their "toy-like" quality—they bore little resemblance to any recognizable prototype—but they later became larger and more elaborate, featuring cast-iron bodies like those he had used on his earlier floor trains. By 1910, when the proportions and outlines of the firm's trains had much improved, Ives had begun to produce electric-powered models of trains in American outline, at first in Gauge "0" and, from 1912 onward, in Gauge "1".

AMERICAN FLYER

The Ives company, under its slogan "Ives Toys make Happy Boys", continued to prosper after its founder's death in 1918, although its Gauge "1" models were eclipsed by the introduction of Lionel's "American Standard Gauge" trains (see below). However, the market crash of 1929 resulted in the takeover of Ives by its major competitors, American Flyer, Hafner, and Lionel, and all trading under the Ives' name ceased in 1931.

The fierce competition that was waged in Germany and in the export markets by such firms as Bing, Märklin, Carette, Bub, and other prominent makers, was mirrored in the United States in the first decades of the century by the rivalry between Ives and American Flyer. The latter company was largely the creation of William F. Hafner (who left it to begin a model railway business under his own name in 1913-14), and it began to manufacture clockwork trains in 1907, and electric trains from 1915-16. Many of American Flyer's products were similar to those of Ives, notably a wide range of Gauge "0" trains. The competition between the two companies was soon joined by the toymaking firm founded by Joshua Lionel Cowen, which was to become known simply as Lionel.

THE LIONEL COMPANY

The Lionel Manufacturing Company was established in New York by 1906, and its earliest products of note were electric tramcars in a gauge approximating to Gauge "3". Upon beginning to produce models in Gauge "0", however, Lionel found itself in competition not only with Ives and American Flyer, but also with the Nuremburg makers whose toys were by this time flooding the American market. Cowen therefore decided to attempt to find a market for larger-size models and, after studying the Gauge "2" items of Bing and Märklin, decided on a similar size. It is sometimes said to have been the result of a design error that his gauge turned out to be 2·125in (54mm) measured between the inner sides of the rails, and thus somewhat above the standard Gauge "2", measured from the centres of the rails, then established by the German makers; but it may equally well have been a deliberate ploy to ensure that those who purchased his locomotives and track would not be able to use them with the products of his rivals, but would also have to purchase his own rolling stock and accessories. Whatever the truth of the matter, it was in this manner that the "American Standard Gauge", as Lionel's 2·125in (54mm) gauge was to become known, was created; and at about the same time "Lionel Lines" became the trademark of the company.

Lionel issued a number of steam-outline locomotives, all electrically-propelled, in its new Standard Gauge, among them a very presentable American-style 4-4-0 of tinplate construction throughout (as opposed to Ives' cast-iron locomotives), as well as a number of tinplate tramcars. (It is worthwhile noting at this point that Lionel registered the term "Standard Gauge" at the US Patent Office in 1915, but, to confuse the issue, referred also to its Gauge "0" trains as "Standard Gauge" items.)

In 1912 there appeared from Lionel, in the 2·125in (54mm) Standard Gauge, some electric-outline, electric-powered locomotives loosely based on prototypes of the New York Central and Hudson River Railroad. The earlier examples were very simple, with 0-4-0 wheel arrangement, and bore little resemblance to their prototypes. Later, however, there was added to the range a large and very impressive locomotive fitted with two bogies and of very strong construction. This was a very popular model and, along with the success of the firm's tinplate tramcars, firmly established Lionel as a powerful force in the American market.

That same market had, from around 1912, also attracted increased efforts from Bing and Märklin, who now began to make electric-outline trains in Gauge "0" and "1", with either electric or clockwork propulsion, specifically for the American market. Bing even produced some locomotives with cast-iron bodies in the style favoured by some American makers. But production of all these trains, which were strongly influenced in style by the products of Ives and Lionel, was of fairly short duration, ending in 1914 with the outbreak of World War I and not being resumed thereafter.

HORNBY GAUGE "0"

To return now to the British scene. As I have already mentioned, after World War II Hornby produced a new range of Gauge "0" trains, beginning in 1947, but these were only of the simpler type, consisting of 0-4-0 locomotives and four-wheeled coaches and wagons. Although the firm had, in 1946, advertised for sale some of the favourite pre-War items, it is certain that these were from pre-War stock and that the best of the Gauge "0" range was not put back into production

after World War II. Instead, Hornby decided to concentrate on the Dublo (Gauge "00") range, which had now become very popular, since Gauge "00" was, in terms of the space needed for a layout, much more practical than Gauge "0", and the Dublo models were generally much more realistic and faithful to prototype than Hornby's larger models.

However, after World War II Hornby also carried on with its simple Gauge "0" sets, all in clockwork, made in the colours of the four major pre-nationali-

Above: *Gauge "1" 4-6-0 "Lord Nelson" Locomotive and Eight-Wheeled (two bogies) Tender, numbered "736", by Gebrüder Märklin, Germany, dating from the late 1920s. This massive spirit-fired steam locomotive provides a typical example of Märklin's complete disregard of truth-to-prototype—but also displays the endearing "toy-like" quality of the firm's models. Catalogued in Great Britain by Gamage's in 1929 only, at a price of £8 8s 0d (£8.40, $10.08), it was then cheekily described as a "perfect reproduction of the Southern Railway Company's 'Lord Nelson'". Made in Gauge "1" only, and in very small numbers, it was not a commercial success and is now extremely rare—one of the most sought-after collector's items. The example shown here has a Bing tender: it was discovered by the author some 20 years ago, minus its tender, which had been destroyed in a fire. Length (engine and tender): 26·5in (67·31cm).*

Left: *Boxed Train Set by Gebrüder Bing, Nuremburg, Germany, dating from before World War I. This charming little unpowered floor train consists of a locomotive approximately of Precursor type and five coaches, made in what approximates to the modern Gauge "N". This example is lithographed in London and North-Western Railway (L&NWR) livery, but it was also made in other liveries in shades of blue and green. This is a desirable item, especially, as shown here, with its original box. Note that, for once, the illustration on the box lid is not too far removed from what the buyer would actually find inside the box! It was, understandably enough, the policy of most toy-makers (certainly not just the makers of toy trains) to illustrate their boxes in a grand and dramatic manner—and for all that the boxes are today, like their contents, collector's items, there must have been many children who were disappointed when they viewed what lay beneath the colourful lids. Length (engine and tender: 5·00in (12·7cm); (coach): 3·25in (8·25cm).*

sation British railway companies (LMS, LNER, GWR, and SR) and, soon after nationalisation, in British Railways (BR; later called British Rail) colours. Some of the stations and accessories of pre-War type also became available once more, albeit most in very simplified form. This limited Gauge "0" series ambled along through the 1950s, but by the end of that decade many of its items had been deleted, and Gauge "0" production ceased altogether in 1965.

HORNBY DUBLO

The story of Hornby Dublo (a registered trade name for the Hornby company's Gauge "00" items) was quite different. The origins of Gauge "00" are dealt with below, but so far as Hornby is concerned the Dublo range was introduced in 1938 with the issue of two diecast LNER locomotives—the streamlined A.4 Pacific "Sir Nigel Gresley" and an N.2 Class 0-6-2 Tank Engine—both of which were available in clockwork or electric, with tinplate track to suit either means of propulsion. Lithographed tinplate LNER coaches, including an articulated unit, were also available, along with various vans and open wagons.

As with Gauge "0", the Dublo range was marketed both in boxed sets, complete with track, or as separate items. Such accessories as stations, signals, and tunnels were soon to be had, and before production halted in 1940, electrically-operated points, engine sheds, and new wagons had been added to the range.

After World War II, Hornby Dublo production recommenced in 1947. The pre-War items were again available, with the addition of a "Duchess" Class Pacific locomotive of the LMS, with maroon bogie coaches in tinplate. Gauge "0" was now rapidly waning in popularity and "00" was becoming the fashionable gauge. Since it took up only about half the space of Gauge "0", a fairly comprehensive "00" layout could be accommodated on the average dining-room table—an important consideration in the smaller, compact houses that were being built in Britain after World War II.

So popular did Hornby Dublo become that, in the immediate post-War years, when there was a general shortage of raw materials for manufacture, demand often outstripped supply, and it was not until the early 1950s that more new items were added to the range. In 1953 the old railway company colours were discontinued, and all models thereafter appeared in British Railways livery.

By the later 1950s, the Hornby Dublo Catalogue listed up to a dozen steam-outline locomotives and a diesel, and wagons and coaches of plastic or

Above: *Gauge "1" (above) and Gauge "0" (below) Motor Car Traffic Vans—see also (4), pages 44-45—from the series of 1909 made by Carette, Nuremburg, Germany, for sale in Great Britain by Bassett-Lowke. They were modelled on a prototype made for the automobile coach fitter Mulliner, famous for its bodies for Rolls Royce cars. Both these vans are lettered for the London and North-Western Railway (L&NWR), both are numbered "13445" and bear also the words "For Motor Car Traffic". Both also carry on their ends the legend: "Mulliner, Long Acre, London and Northampton". The photograph well illustrates the considerable difference in size* between the two gauges; the van was also produced in Gauge "2". Although most Carette wagons and vans are, generally, not too hard for the collector to find, this item is fairly rare in Gauge "1" and very rare in Gauge "0". It is, in fact, not uncommon for Gauge "0" items, although produced in far greater numbers, to be rarer than their Gauge "1" equivalents. This, the author believes, is because children were allowed to play unsupervised with Gauge "0" items, which thus got hard usage, whereas the larger and more expensive Gauge "1" models were played with under parental supervision. Lengths (Gauge "1"): 9·75in (24·765cm); (Gauge "0"): 7in (17·78cm).

part-plastic construction had begun to appear. From about that time, however, sales began to decline. In 1965 Hornby was taken over by Triang (Lines Brothers), and that firm initially incorporated some items from the Dublo range into its catalogue.

MODERN GERMAN MAKERS

However, although the mid-1960s saw the eclipse of Hornby, makers of Gauge "00" railways elsewhere were by no means in the same trouble. In Germany, Fleischmann, and our old friends Märklin of Göppingen in particular, were surging ahead and actually increasing their sales of finely-made, highly-detailed models of locomotives and rolling stock, many items being of European outline. Many of these models remain in production today, and the discontinued models of the 1950s-1970s period are not too difficult for collectors to find.

The modern products of such makers as Fleischmann and Märklin are a delight to run, and purely from the collector's point of view their attractive appearance, enhanced by such detail as the near-watchmaker's precision of the valve gear on the locomotives, will ensure their becoming collector's items of the future. (Märklin, incidentally, still makes a first-rate range of electrically-powered locomotives, with rolling stock, in Gauge "1".) Another

Above: *Gauge "0" 4-4-4 Tank Engine (above), and 0-6-0 Tank Engine (below); "controlled clockwork" models made in the late 1940s by Van Reimsdijk Clockwork Mechanisms, Great Britain. The specially-constructed, long-running, variable-speed mechanism fitted in these locomotives is controlled by a governor, operated by a lever in the cab, which enables them to run realistically at a very slow speed. Van Reimsdijk initially made a number of trams in Gauge "0", and in about 1947 the firm received an order from H.M. Sell of Bassett-Lowke for a quality of locomotives in Gauge "00", then at the peak of its popularity. These proved very successful,* and more than 3,000 were made. At that time, a large number of indifferently-made Gauge "0" toy trains were being produced in Great Britain by such companies as Chad Valley and Brimtoy. It was felt that there would be a market for a better-quality product, and so the 4-4-4 Tank Locomotive seen here (above) was designed: some 600 were made and they were sold principally by the large London stores of Hamley's, Gamage's, and Selfridge. The 0-6-0 Tank Locomotive (below) had a production run of 1,000; it was made to the order of Walker and Holtzapfel, a firm still in business as W&H Models. Lengths (4-4-4): 11·125in (28·25cm); (0-6-0): 8·75in (22·225cm).

German maker still in production with finely-made locomotives in Gauge "00" is Arnold, famous in the inter-War years for its tinplate boats and stationary steam engines.

ORIGINS OF GAUGE "00"

While still on the subject of Gauge "00" and German makers, it should be mentioned that although Hornby Dublo has become almost synonymous with that gauge to British, French, and many American enthusiasts, Hornby was in fact a relatively latecomer to the Gauge "00" scene. As early as 1922, at the request of Bassett-Lowke, Gebrüder Bing produced the "Bing Table-Top Railway", the first commercially-produced Gauge "00" range. Its components, all in tinplate, were small 2-4-0 tank engines and 2-4-0 tender locomotives, with four-wheeled carriages and wagons, complete with printed tinplate track. At first the Table-Top Railways were made in clockwork only, but three-rail electric propulsion was later available, as was an attractive array of accessories, including stations, signal box, engine shed, level crossing (grade crossing), signals, tunnel, and telegraph poles.

Wenman J. Bassett-Lowke's request to Bing was largely dictated by changing social circumstances. After World War I, the British tended to live in more compact houses (a similar factor operated after World War II, as already mentioned), and apartment buildings, with their small rooms, became increasingly popular. Even Gauge "0" railways, small as they were in comparison with the earlier popular Gauges "1" and "2", took up too much room in restricted accommodation, and Bassett-Lowke, with his usual flair, recognized the need for a smaller commercially-made gauge.

It is worth repeating what he said on the subject in later years:

"When builders were steadily putting up more compact houses with smaller rooms, I visualised the demand for a still narrower gauge than "0", and I brought over from Germany the first model railway outfit of just half that size on a gauge of ⅝" (0·625in, 16mm). It was a crude affair made of tin. But this introduction to Great Britain of Gauge "00" marked an important milestone in model railway history."

TRIX TWIN RAILWAYS

A further development in the Gauge "00" story took place in Germany in the mid-1930s. Again, one of the Bing family was concerned, and again Bassett-Lowke was responsible for introducing

Left: *4-6-2 Locomotive by Buddy "L" (The Moline Pressed Steel Company, East Moline, Illinois), USA. It is difficult for a photograph to do justice to this huge and magnificent push-along engine, which is possibly the largest metal toy locomotive ever made commercially. This is one of the range of super-robust toys made during the 1920s-30s by the Moline company. The series was created by Fred Lundahl, president of the company, who in 1920 had the idea of making a toy truck from scrap metal for his son, Buddy. The popularity of the truck led to the inception of the series. The locomotive is of heavy steel plate, with sprung cast-iron wheels. A number of different freight cars and a caboose were made and, later, steel track. American collectors have nicknamed it "The Brute". Length: 42in (106·68cm).*

Above: *Gauge "0" Goods Train, a boxed set by Hornby, Great Britain, dating from about 1947. At this time, soon after World War II, Hornby was again producing train sets, but with 0-4-0 locomotives and four-wheeled rolling stock only. Note the striking difference between the illustration on the lid and the actual contents of the box: this dichotomy dates from the earliest train sets—the purchaser rarely got what was shown on the lid! However, the small clockwork locomotive, numbered "5689" and in London, Midland & Scottish Railway (LMS) livery, is by no means unattractive, and is complete with four-wheeled tender, a flat wagon, an open wagon, a guards van and an oval of tinplate track. Hornby's better Gauge "0" items did not reappear after World War II, when the company concentrated on its Gauge "00" range.*

the new development into Britain. This was the range first known as "Trix Express", to become best-known as "Trix Twin", introduced by Stefan Bing (who had left the Bing family firm in the later 1920s), with the encouragement of Bassett-Lowke, and first appearing in 1935. Trix introduced an ingenious system which permitted "two electric trains running on the same line at different speeds".

At first, Trix trains were of German outline. In 1938, however, a division occurred in the firm when Stefan Bing and his original partners were replaced by directors approved by the Nazi regime. Bing and his associates moved to Britain, where a Trix manufactory was established under the auspices of Bassett-Lowke. Both the German and British Trix operations resumed production after World War II, and the latter produced a number of British-outline trains, culminating in a very presentable Pacific locomotive and a "Coronation Streamliner". British

Trix continued to make Gauge "00" electric trains until the mid-1960s; the West Germany Trix company, as mentioned below, carried on into the age of gauges smaller even than "00".

SMALLER GAUGES

Gauge "00" proved to be by no means the smallest gauge for commercially-made model railways. In the late 1960s there appeared in Great Britain from the toymaking firm of Lone Star a number of diecast trains, unpowered "push-along" models, in a size approximating to what was to become known as "N" Gauge. A year or two later, the German firm of Arnold produced an electric train running on track 0·35in (9mm) wide, about half the size of Gauge "00"—and thus "N" Gauge arrived.

Märklin, Fleischmann, and Minitrix (a branch of the West German Trix company) were quick to join the "N" Gauge scene, and the popularity of this mini-gauge quickly increased until

today "N" Gauge models, which permit elaborate and complex layouts to be constructed in a very small space, can be bought from most toyshops.

To carry matters to the extreme, Märklin has since produced an absolutely minute system, running on 0·256in (6·5mm) track, and called it "Z" Gauge. With this system, the enthusiast can literally run a train around a soup plate or build an extensive layout on a coffee table! "Z" Gauge is, perhaps, just a little too small for real enjoyment in the running, but it is nevertheless a fascinating novelty.

GAUGE "1" TODAY

Almost in reaction to the brief account of mini-gauges above, I will mention at this point the increasing contemporary interest in both Europe

Above: *Gauge "O" 4-6-2 "Flying Scotsman" Locomotive, numbered "4472", and Eight-Wheeled Tender, in London and North Eastern Railway (LNER) livery, made by Winteringham, Northampton, England, for Bassett-Lowke, Great Britain. One of the most popular of all Bassett-Lowke's locomotives, this model was available in clockwork or electric from the early 1930s until World War II; it was reissued post-War, first in LNER colours and numbered "103", then in British Railways (BR) blue livery, and finally in BR green. The example shown is an electric version dating from the late 1930s; models incorporating various styles of mechanism are to be found, the worst mechanically being the early side-geared types. For an all-lithographed locomotive, this had a most realistic appearance and, with its companion "Royal Scot", seemed to mark a better approach to scale by Bassett-Lowke. Note, however, that the appearance of the example shown here has been enhanced by the present owner, who has made subtle additions to the front end:* such modifications are acceptable to collectors if they are capable of easy removal to restore the model to its original state. "Flying Scotsman" is shown here with an LNER Dining Saloon made by Exley, Great Britain, and marketed both by the maker and by Bassett-Lowke. It is one of the better-looking LNER vehicles made by Exley before World War II: some look truly appalling because of the maker's attempt to simulate varnished teak. Exley's pre-War vehicles usually have aluminium body wrappers, cast ends, wooden floors, real glass windows and card interiors (ie, detail of seats, dividers etc). It is interesting to compare this Winteringham/ Bassett-Lowke "Flying Scotsman" with the contemporary Hornby version shown at (7), pages 42-43; the latter, apart from the correct number "4472", has almost nothing in common with its prototype. An equally unconvincing version by Bowman, Great Britain, is shown at (2), pages 96-97. Lengths (engine and tender): 20·25in (51·435cm); (coach): 16·5in (41·91cm).

and the United States in the collecting and running of trains in Gauge "1". In Britain, there has for some years been a devoted band of enthusiasts for this gauge, operating under the banner of the Gauge "1" Association. Many of its members are skilled model engineers whose interest lies in building and running their own trains rather than in collecting; but not a few are, like myself, enthusiasts who love both collecting trains and running them.

The Gauge "1" scene received a tremendous boost in 1975, when the Japanese firm of Aster brought out a high-pressure steam model of the British Southern Railway's "Schools" Class locomotive "Winchester". This is shown, with other Aster models, on *pages 116-117* (and it is interesting to note that the example photographed

for this book, from the author's collection, is in fact the original model). This well-designed, finely-proportioned locomotive was, above all, an excellent runner, and it was soon followed by a number of other fine locomotives, including an American Wild-West type 4-4-0 "Reno", an intriguing Shay logging locomotive, and a PLM Pacific.

Since 1975, Aster has produced some twenty different models in American, British, and Continental outlines—and special mention must be made of the company's truly awesome "Big Boy", a model of one of the most famous American locomotives, which is more than 47in (120cm) long and weighs around 42lb (19kg). It is a magnificent sight to see it working. The Aster company is still in production, its latest offering being a handsome

pages 116-117

Above: *Gauge "0" "Flèche d'Or" ("Golden Arrow") Train Set by Hornby, dating from the late 1930s. The romance of the Paris-London express passenger service is finely captured in this beautiful set, which consists of an Atlantic Locomotive and Tender made in the French Hornby factory at Bobigny-Seine, and two No 2 Special Pullmans, made by Hornby, Liverpool, Great Britain, but painted in France for inclusion in the set. This example is in superb condition, complete down to its original guarantee—although the 20-volt electric control unit is probably a post-World War II item. A similar "Blue Train" set—see pages 78-79—was marketed; both French-made sets came in boxes bearing the striking logo seen here. The sets appeared also in clockwork, but most of the more exotic French-made sets seem to be electric models. The 4-4-2 locomotive and eight-wheeled tender are in "Nord" finish and both are numbered "31801". Lengths (engine and tender): 16·5in (41·91cm); (coach): 13in (33·02cm).*

Right: *Gauge "0" M Series "Silver Jubilee" Train Set by Hornby, Great Britain, dating from the late 1930s. The LNER's famous streamlined train was an obvious choice for Hornby's cheap M Series: the little locomotive, in non-reversing clockwork only, came complete with tender, articulated coach set, and 9in (22·86cm) radius track with very sharp curves. The lithographed, boxed set was priced at around 5s 6d (27½p, 33c). The set also appeared in strange colour combinations of maroon-and-cream and shades of green. In good condition and with the original box, these sets are now quite hard to find. Length (overall): 17in (43·18cm).*

Far right: *Gauge "0" 4-6-2 "Princess Elizabeth" Locomotive, numbered "6201", and Six-Wheeled Tender, in London, Midland & Scottish Railway (LMS) livery, by Hornby, Great Britain, issued early in 1937 and in production only until World War II. With this representation of a "Princess Royal Class" locomotive designed by Sir William Stanier for the LMS, Hornby broke away from the four-coupled mechanism and produced its largest and most expensive model locomotive, available in electric only and priced at £5 5s 0d (£5.25, $6.30). Although it embodied certain inaccuracies forced upon the maker by the radius of the track on which it was intended to run, this was a beautifully-made and finished model and, as seen here, was sold in a special presentation box. Although a surprising number of Hornby "Princesses" are extant, boxed models in good condition are avidly sought after by collectors. The author purchased one of these locomotives (not the example shown here, which is the property of Chris Littledale, The British Engineerium Museum, Hove, Sussex) in the 1950s for the then quite considerable sum of £7.00 ($8.40)—it would cost very much more today! Length (engine and tender): 20·5in (52·07cm).*

three-cylinder "Mallard" of the LNER —see (1), *pages 118-119.* And although Aster locomotives are, perhaps, best described as being intended for adult enthusiasts, rather than being toys in the proper sense, they are excellent working models and they are certainly destined to be among the collector's items of the future.

FUTURE COLLECTABLES

Other railway items currently available from firms in production today include the products of the Italian firm Lima, which offers a wide selection of trains in both Gauge "0" and Gauge "00". The Gauge "00" models of the Italian maker Rivarossi are probably also worth the attention of the collector with an eye to the future. The great and famous West German firm of Märklin is, as I have mentioned, still producing trains in Gauges "1", "00", and "Z". The name of the West German maker Lehmann, established in the late 19th century and long familiar to toy collectors all over the world, appears on the currently-popular "L.G.B. Railway", which is made in approximately 0·5in (12·7mm) scale and runs on Gauge "1" track; in other words, it is Gauge "1" narrow gauge.

THE COLLECTING HOBBY

The passion for collecting toy and model trains (as opposed to the hobby of running them: the difference between the two attitudes is touched on below) appears first to have achieved significant expression in the United States of America in the early 1930s. By 1935, a band of American enthusiasts had combined to produce the "Model Railroader's Digest", the first magazine devoted largely to the interests of toy railway collectors. A major contributor to the journal, and a leading figure in the collecting movement, was Louis Hertz, who was later to write a number of books that would become standard works of reference for the model railway devotee (see the list of "Reference Books" at the end of this introduction).

In Great Britain and on the European continent, at that time, there seems to have been a comparatively small number of collectors, pursuing their hobby in isolation: no printed material, specialist magazines and the like, devoted to the collecting pursuit (as opposed to running or building model railways) seems to have appeared before 1939. However, in the early post-War years, examination of the columns of "Sales and Wants" in the

"Model Railway News" reveals items indicating that the collecting of tinplate trains was then beginning to attract increasing interest.

It was about this time that I began to collect toy trains, inspired by a chance visit to a junk-shop where I found a Bowman steam locomotive—see (5), *pages 96-97*—identical to the one I had possessed when a child. This little toy was only about 7in (18cm) long; it was a kind of diminutive tank engine, with four wheels and a single oscillating cylinder in the cab. The sight of it brought back nostalgic memories of burnt fingers (not to mention burnt carpets!) and the smell of methylated spirit and burning oil.

BRITISH COLLECTORS

As the collecting hobby began to gain increasing impetus in the United Kingdom, specialist dealers, some dealing exclusively in tinplate trains, began to appear on the scene. An early practitioner in this field was John Proctor of Patcham, near Brighton, Sussex, who regularly contributed humorous advertisements to the "Model Railway News" in the later 1950s and throughout the 1960s. Veteran British collectors will fondly remember that

his garden shed was a veritable Aladdin's cave of toy train goodies! Other dealers early on the British collecting scene included Cherry's of Richmond, Surrey; Molden of Hammersmith, London; Jonathan Minns; and "Steam Age" of London.

In the 1950s and early 1960s, the toy train collecting hobby in Great Britain was a gentle and civilized pursuit and prices were generally modest. At the risk of breaking the hearts of collectors who have come more recently into the field, I will list a few of the items I purchased for my collection, with their prices, in the 1950s. They included: a mint-condition Gauge "0" "Flying Scotsman" by Bassett-Lowke—see *pages 25-26*—for £8 ($9.60); a Hornby "Princess Elizabeth"—see illustration above—for £7 ($8.40); a rare Gauge "1" "Sir Alexander" by Bing—see (4), *pages 48-49*—for £12 ($14.40); and a beautiful mint, boxed, Gauge "1" London, Brighton and South Coast Railway Tank Engine by Bing—see (6), *pages 58-59*—for £15 ($18.00). As we all know to our cost, prices are very different today!

The years following World War II saw, both in Europe and the United States, a tremendous upsurge of interest in "antiques" and "bygones", in "collectable" objects, generally—and it was inevitable that toy trains, with their overwhelming nostalgic appeal (for we all remember the trains of our childhood), should be caught up in this tide of enthusiasm. (In this context, it is interesting to note that collectable toy trains are universally regarded as "antiques", although very few of them meet the formerly accepted criterion for that designation of being more than one hundred years old.)

THE PRICE EXPLOSION

The rise of collectors' interest in toy trains was, sooner or later, bound to be reflected on the auction scene and, in Great Britain, it is possible exactly to date the beginning of the "modern era", with its high prices, in railway collecting. On Wednesday, 5 October 1966, the international auction house of Christie's held a sale at "ten thirty o'clock" in its "Great Rooms" in St James's, London. Organized by Jonathan Minns, who has already been mentioned as a pioneer in British toy train collecting, and Patrick Lindsay, a director of Christie's, it was of "Fine Historical Steam Engine Models and Ship Models". Although, as that

catalogue title suggests, it largely featured fine, hand-crafted, large-scale locomotives, ships stationary steam engines, and the like, it also included a few tinplate trains, as well as a fair number of examples of the ubiquitous "piddler" locomotive.

The prices paid at that first historic sale for tinplate trains from Bassett-Lowke make interesting reading; eg, £65 ($78.00) for a Gauge "0" 2-6-4 Baltic Tank Locomotive. Although very cheap by today's standards, they were by no means a give-away in terms of the mid-1960s—and were certainly high enough to indicate that tinplate train collecting was now an important market. Subsequent sales confirmed this: prices rocketed, to reach a peak around 1970. Since that time, price increases, although seemingly steep, have been more or less in line with inflation—although this does not apply to the rarer, most sought-after, items, such as trains and boats by Märklin, some of which have exceeded their sale-room estimates by a factor of six times or more.

BUYING TOY TRAINS

However, the would-be collector, apprehensive of London's West End or

New York's Fifth Avenue prices, need not despair of finding items at more reasonable cost. Today, many auctions devoted to toy trains are held not only by the major international auction houses, but also by many smaller ones. There are, too, all over the United States, Britain, and in some other countries, regular "swap-meets", where enthusiasts gather to buy, sell, or exchange material. These are fruitful venues for the beginning collector of modest tastes, who will be able to acquire items at prices that will not empty his pockets. However, if his taste is for the rare and exotic, prices are likely to be high everywhere.

In both Europe and the United States there are specialist magazines and gazettes for the collector, some with a very recent publication history, and it is well worth studying the "For Sale" columns of these. Also, the novice should not be shy of visiting specialist dealers: although their wares will generally not be cheap, the sensible buyer will usually get good value for his money if he patronizes a reputable dealer.

Some people may believe that a dealer's "mark-up"—ie, the price he asks for an item above what he paid for it—is likely to be excessive, but it should be remembered that the dealer usually has to find his stock through expensive advertising and that he may well face other large "overheads", including the rent and maintenance of his premises. Buying from a reputable dealer is, in any case, perhaps the easiest and safest way to collect—and an experienced, knowledgeable dealer will often be prepared to give a good deal of useful advice to his customers.

COLLECTORS' CHOICES

So much for where to collect: but *what* to collect? One's personal preference will be the first deciding factor, but there are other vital considerations that will influence the choice. How much space is available to keep and display the collection? And, of course, how much can you afford to spend on your hobby?

You may choose to specialize in the work of one particular maker; in items in one particular gauge; or even in the products of one famous maker over a limited period of time. For example, I known an enthusiast in Holland who collects only trains made by Bing up to the year 1900. That kind of collection would suit someone who has limited space—and plenty of money! But every serious collector will, whatever the pressures upon him of time, space,

Left: *In the mid-to-late 1930s, Bassett-Lowke, Great Britain, produced Gauge "0" models in electric (as shown) and clockwork of streamlined 4-6-2 locomotives of the London, Midland & Scottish Railway (LMS) and London and North Eastern Railway (LNER). These models with eight-wheeled corridor tenders are now very rare— only about 200 of the LNER versions were made—and the LNER locomotive seen here in the process of restoration by its present owner (Chris Littledale, a notable professional restorer of tinplate toys) is the rarest model of them all. The name-plates apparent at the front end are non-original and will be removed, and the locomotive will be restored to its original "Silver Link" shades of grey: the LNER versions also appeared in garter-blue livery as "Empire of India" and "Dominion of Canada". Since these models were almost entirely hand-made, with limited press-work, the price was very high for those days, at around £13 13s 0d (£13.65, $16.38). Length (engine and tender): 20in (50·8cm).*

Above: *Gauge "00" "Sir Nigel Gresley" Train Set by Hornby Dublo, Great Britain. The late 1930s marked the Hornby company's venture into Gauge "00", which was to supplant Gauge "0". The earlier Hornby Dublo (ie, "Double 0", "00") models were made in both clockwork and electric, and this photograph shows a most desirable boxed set in clockwork. Apart from its mechanism, the "Sir Nigel Gresley" 4-6-2 locomotive, with its eight-wheeled corridor tender, is distinguished as a pre-World War II example by the valance over the wheels and by the number "4498": the locomotive reappeared post-War numbered "7", and in electric only. Note the contemporary instruction and advertising leaflets. In the 1930s, this set was priced at £3 10s 0d (£3.50, $4.20) in electric, or £1 19s 6d (£1.97½, $2.37) in clockwork; the coaches, of typical LNER articulated type, were also available separately, as a unit only, at a price of 6s 6d (32½p, 39c). Lengths (engine and tender): 11·125in (28·26cm); (coach unit): 15·125in (38·42cm).*

or expense, form his own preferences; so perhaps the best I can do at this point is to say something of my own collecting experience.

Personally, I like to collect a bit of everything! My collection of tinplate trains, gathered together over a period of some forty years, consists of items in Gauges "0", "1", "2", "3", and "4", powered by live steam, clockwork, and electric—with a few "push-alongs" for good measure. Most were made before World War II; in fact, a large proportion dates from before World War I. As you will see when you look through the photographic spreads in this book, all the great makers are represented—Bing, Märklin, Carette, Bassett-Lowke, and the rest (some of the Hornby items, too, are mine, but the majority of these come from the collection of my friend Chris Littledale,

a Hornby specialist), along with many items by less wellknown makers. I have always collected what I *like*, regardless of fashions in the collecting world—and that, for me, is one of the secrets of a truly satisfying collection.

RUNNING: A PERSONAL VIEW

Unlike many collectors who are content to have their pieces impressively arranged on shelves or displayed in glass cases, I like my trains to run—and most of them do. They spend much of their time nicely displayed on shelves, of course, since every collector likes to have his treasures on show for his own visual delight and that of visitors, but beneath these shelves, at table-top height, I have an extensive rail layout running all around my large "train-room". The Gauge "0" and Gauge "1" tracks are of fairly coarse

scale, so that I can run models ranging from, say, a Bing locomotive of 1895 vintage to a Japanese-made Aster locomotive of 1985. In fact, as I write these words, Märklin's Gauge "1" 4-6-2 PLM Pacific of *c*1912—see (1), *pages 68-69*—is steaming scale-mile after scale-mile around me!

To me, nothing looks (or sounds) so magnificent, nor brings the collecting pursuit so vividly alive, as the sight and sound of a vintage methylated-spirit-fired Märklin locomotive chugging along with a rake of period coaches rattling behind. I believe that this is what collecting is all about—and I know from my own experience over the years that it is always possible to run trains, even if only modestly and in the smaller gauges when space is very limited. It is the way to full enjoyment of one's collection.

Many of my friends in the collecting fraternity believe that I'm crazy to subject very rare and valuable items by such makers as Märklin to further wear by steaming them—but I have never let the reputed financial value of any of my trains prevent me from getting them into working order and really enjoying them. I get little pleasure from purely "shelf" items. You will sometimes find that a distinction is made in the collecting world—I have occasionally made it myself in the captions that accompany the photographs in this book—between toy train "collectors", implying that these collect mainly for display, and "runners", whose interest lies mainly in operating their trains. I can't make such a distinction in my own case: I guess I'm a bit of both!

SPECIALIZED COLLECTIONS

To return to the purely collecting aspect, and to areas of specialization: I have a friend, the wellknown British collector David Pressland, whose aim is to collect "the one hundred best toys ever made"—including trains of course. This is an ambition that would daunt most collectors, and it is amazing to record that over a period of about 25 years he has acquired for his collection about fifty items that might well be included in the "hundred best" category, and has written an excellent book, "The Art of the Tin Toy", based on them and other fine specimens.

That, of course, represents the top end of the collecting scale. The beginner today, assuming that he has only a modest amount of money to devote to his hobby, will of necessity begin at the lower end of the scale. Of the various options open to him at this level (and I speak here of both the European and American collecting scenes) he might do worse than to consider specializing in Hornby Gauge "0" material. Hornby items, which were made in both Great Britain and France, are not too difficult to find and, because there is a fair amount of material about, prices are in the main fairly reasonable. However, I should warn the novice collector that some Hornby trains, although not particularly rare, have rocketed in price in recent years and are now expensive.

When I began to collect, immediately after World War II, Hornby items were hardly recognized to be at all collectable, and could be obtained very easily and cheaply. But as the prices fetched by

Above: *Gauge "0" Steam Train by Mamod, Great Britain; a recent addition to the model railway scene, first made in 1979 and still in production. The 0-4-0 Locomotive and the two wagons, as shown here, are sold as a boxed set together with an oval of narrow-gauge iron track and a box of solid fuel tablets (also shown). Originally Mamod engines were methylated spirit-fired, but after a number of accidents were reported the company switched to solid fuel in the mid-1970s. The Mamod company was set up in the 1930s by Geoffrey Malins, and until 1939, and again after World War II, made a range of stationary steam engines suitable for driving Meccano models. Later, a number of steam-driven road vehicles were added to the range, culminating in a massive Foden Steam Wagon and a splendid Steam Roadster; the latter, modelled on an automobile of c1910, was full of nostalgic period charm. Like most toymakers all over the world, Mamod has had to weather financial crises in recent years; it has fortunately survived and even plans some new models for the future. So far as the collector of toy trains is concerned, this Mamod train set falls into much the same category as the Gauge "3½" "Stephenson's Rocket" steam train set by Hornby, another currently available item, shown on page 8. It will obviously be of the greatest appeal to those whose major interest lies in operating toy trains—and, unlike the much larger Hornby set, this is well-suited to indoor running—and it is probably best described as a toy that may well prove to be a "future collectable".*

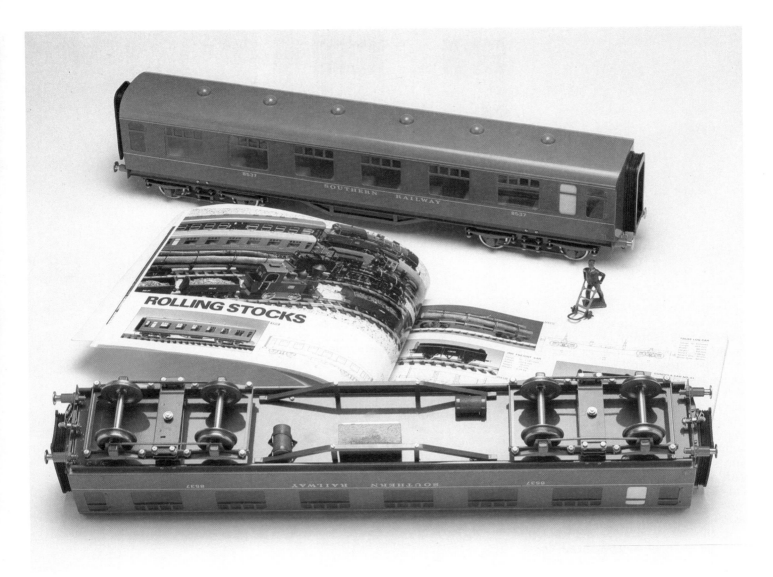

Above: *Gauge "1" Southern Railway Passenger Coaches by Aster, Japan; shown with the Aster Catalogue in which they are listed. These were made to run with Aster's "Schools Class" locomotive "Winchester"—fully described at (2), pages 116-117—and first appeared in 1975. They were made only for a brief period and in small numbers and have now become fairly rare collector's items. Strongly constructed from sheet brass, with steel bogies and turned cast-iron wheels, the attractively-finished coaches are fitted with sprung buffers, sprung three-link couplings, and dummy corridor connections. The underside of one is shown here to demonstrate the bogie arrangement, underframe fittings, and the nut-and-bolt construction that allows them to be disassembled (although the author has no knowledge of their being available in kit form). The less-than-scale length—21in (53cm)—that allows them to negotiate sharp curves on the track is an interesting throwback to the days of Carette and Bing, and they display some of the "toy-like" quality of their German-made predecessors. Although these coaches had only a short production run, the Aster company is still very much in operation. Its trains, probably best described as expensive toys for adults, appeal particularly to collectors who enjoy running as well as displaying trains—and they are certainly "future collectables". A range of Aster locomotives is shown on pages 116-117, and the maker's most recent model, the fine Gauge "1" "Mallard" issued in 1984, is shown at (1), pages 118-119.*

the products of the great toy train makers of Germany—Bing, Carette, and Märklin—have risen enormously, and as more and more collectors have come into the field to compete for these items (and, paradoxically, it seems that the higher prices go, the more public interest is aroused, and even more collectors join the competition!), so newcomers have turned to reasonably-priced alternatives such as Hornby, with the result that Hornby material has become fashionable and its price, too, has risen.

BUYING HORNBY TRAINS

Nevertheless, many items by Hornby (and by some other good makers outside the German "big three") may still be acquired at quite reasonable prices if the collector goes about it in the right way. It is well worth remembering that it is often cheaper to buy a Hornby item from a reputable specialist dealer, his "mark-up" notwithstanding, than at auction. Often, enthusiasts vie with each other at public auctions to such a pitch of excitement that prices go way over the top. Another good source of material is the various swap-meets which, as I have already mentioned, are held

regularly at many venues: these will be found to be advertised in the various collectors' journals now in circulation. Advertising in these journals (especially, in Britain, in model railway magazines) or in the neighbourhood newspapers for one's "wants" may also prove to be fruitful.

Many most attractive Hornby items dating from after World War II can still be acquired in their original boxes (always a plus point for collectables of any kind), at swap-meets or from dealers, at prices as low as £3-£4 (less than $5.00). But rarer Hornby pieces, particularly those dating from before World War II, will cost quite a bit more. Remember that production of Hornby trains ceased in 1940 and that when the firm started up again in 1946-47; none of the better Gauge "0" items reappeared, either then or later. Thus, any Hornby railway item bearing the "Hornby Series" label, which was used only up to 1940, will be getting on for half-a-century old and will inevitably cost more to acquire.

ELECTRIC RUNNING

Collectors who wish to run their trains as well as display them might do best to seek out Hornby's electric-

driven models. However, my personal preference in Hornby is for clockwork examples: I have always felt that driving a steam-outline train by electricity is a bit of a cheat! Live steam, of course is absolutely authentic—although unavailable in the case of Hornby models—but even a clockwork engine is propelled by the pressure built up by winding the spring; in other words, it runs under its own power, with no help from any exterior source. This is, I suppose, very much a purist view, and it must be said that electric propulsion is clean, easy, and efficient.

If the trains are to be run, the collector will, of course, need track. Hornby tinplate track can be bought very cheaply; it may even be given away if other items are purchased, and Italian-made reproduction track is also available. However, the steel track of larger radius made for the efficient running of such models as the "Princess Elizabeth" is now quite rare and difficult to find.

A COLLECTOR'S CREED

In summing up the fascination that the collecting hobby exerts, and in giving advice on how to obtain the fullest satisfaction from your collection, I can speak only for myself. But perhaps the joy that my collecting activities have brought me over the years is an indication that I have gone about things in the right way; perhaps I am, after all, qualified to pass on some advice.

To my mind, there are three golden rules for the collector. First, buy the best items that your pocket allows—but do not look on your collection as an investment. Tinplate trains of good quality are, of course, likely to appreciate in value, and most collectors will from time to time wish to sell some item—but not so much for monetary profit as to allow for the purchase of some even more desirable specimen. In my experience, dedicated collectors

Above: *Three modern friction-driven floor trains with sparking action; in each case, the skirt showing 4-6-4 wheel arrangement conceals four unflanged wheels. This is an interesting group in that all three locomotives appear to utilize the same body pressing, with different lithography, but all are of different provenance. Number "670" (left) is by Arnold, West Germany; "Silver Link" (centre), marked "Foreign", is probably a pre-War Japanese item; and number "303" is marked "Made in England". Length (each): 5in (12·7cm).*

Right: *The small shunting set in the foreground (note its box, complete with tinplate track, behind it) is a Gauge "0" clockwork train by a Czechoslovakian maker, made for export and dating from c1968. It is of somewhat heavier-gauge metal than most toys of this kind. The "Mountain Express" (centre; its box is in the background) and the "Red Arrow" (right) are both friction-driven floor trains by Japanese makers, dating from c1962 and c1958-59 respectively.*

do rather more swapping, albeit with financial adjustments sometimes, than buying and selling. And the individual who buys and sells merely for financial gain, who speculates in toy trains as he might in stocks and shares, cannot be called a true collector.

Second, in building up your collection, never be afraid to be guided by personal taste rather than by fashion or by the pronouncements of experts. Listen to experienced collectors by all means; study reference books (I have listed some useful titles below); but don't acquire any item just because you feel that you ought to have it—acquire it only if you truly like it.

Third, and most important, remember always that your trains are not only museum specimens but also toys. They are fairly robust—they were made that way to stand the treatment they might get from the children for whom they were intended—and although handling and running them may add a little to their wear, they will not crumble to dust if you take them from their shelves or cases. A collector's "train room' should not be just an art

gallery: it should be full of the sound and smell of live steam, the racket of clockwork, the buzz of electric operation. Your trains were made for children to love and to play with: you will only get complete satisfaction if you do the same—with children, if you can!

REFERENCE BOOKS

I hope that this book will prove to be a useful colour reference guide for collectors everywhere. However, both the beginner and the experienced collector will sometimes need other sources of reference, so I have listed on the right some titles that have proved particularly useful to me, both as a collector and in the compilation of this book. The list is not comprehensive, but I have tried to include both standard reference works and general titles likely to be of use to the novice. The most useful sources of all are likely to be manufacturers' catalogues like those shown on *pages 124-125*, but these may be difficult and expensive to acquire (although some have been reprinted in facsimile and are available in this form from specialist dealers).

Gamage's Christmas Bazaar (UK, 1974)
Alison Aldburgham (ed)

The Collector's Book of the Locomotive (New York, 1966)
Edwin P. Alexander

The Encyclopedia of Model Railways (London, 1979)
Terry Allen (ed)

The Model Railway Handbook (UK, 1942)
W.J. Bassett-Lowke

Early Tinplate Model Railways (London, 1980)
Udo Becher

Model Railways 1838-1939 (London, 1962)
Hamilton Ellis

The Bassett-Lowke Story (London, 1984)
Roland Fuller

Older Locomotives 1900-1942 (London, 1970)
P.G. Gomm

Model Railroading (USA, 1979)
Bruce Greenberg

Toyshop Steam (UK, 1978)
Basil Harley

Riding the Tinplate Rails (USA, 1944)
Messrs Ives of Bridgeport (USA, 1950)
Collecting Model Trains (USA, 1956)
Louis H. Hertz

Die grossen Spurweiten
(The Railway Models of Märklin) (Switzerland, 1969)

Bing, die Modellbahnen unserer Grossväter
(Grandad's Model Railways) (Switzerland. 1972)
Claude Jeanmarie

A Century of Model Trains (London, 1974)
The Great Toys of Georges Carette (London, 1975)
Allen Levy

Model Railway Engines (London, 1969)
J.E. Minns

Mr Gamage's Great Toy Bazaar 1902-1906 (London, 1982)
Charlotte Parry-Crooke (ed)

The Products of Binns Road
(The Hornby Companion Series) (London, 1977)
Peter Randall

Clockwork, Steam and Electric:
The History of Model Railways up to 1939 (UK, 1972)
Gustav Reder

The Golden Age of Toys (Switzerland, 1967)
Jac Remise & Jean Fondin

Bassett-Lowke Railways (London, 1968)
Ian Rutherford Scott, Allen Levy and Roland H. Fuller

The Hornby Book of Trains 1954-1979 (UK, 1979)
S.W. Stevens-Stratten (ed)

History of Model & Miniature Railways (UK Part-Work, 1973-74)
Patrick Whitehouse & John Adams (eds)

The World of Model Trains (London, 1978)
Patrick Whitehouse & Allen Levy (eds)

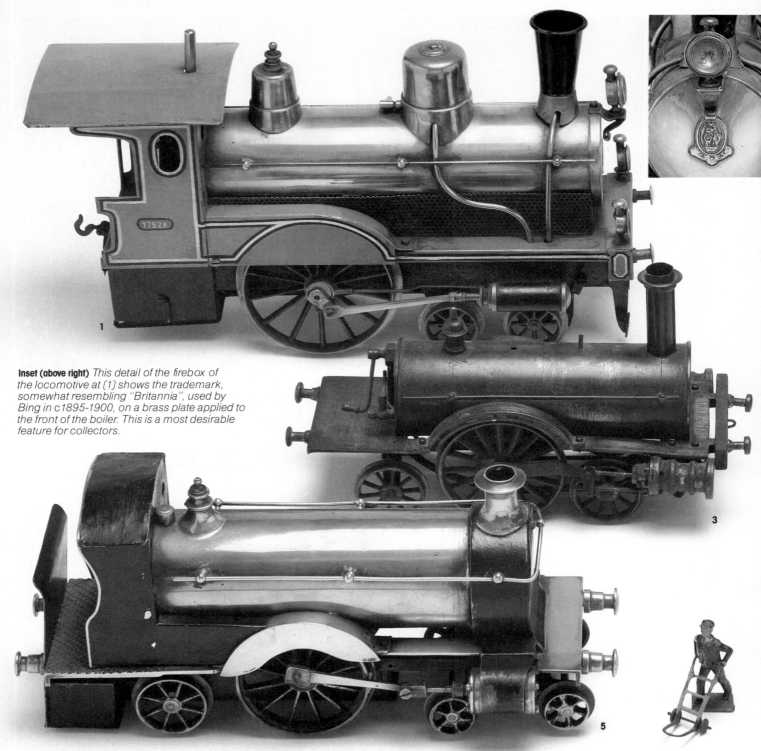

Inset (above right) *This detail of the firebox of the locomotive at (1) shows the trademark, somewhat resembling "Britannia", used by Bing in c1895-1900, on a brass plate applied to the front of the boiler. This is a most desirable feature for collectors.*

1 Gauge "4" 4-2-0 Locomotive, numbered "17528", by Gebrüder Bing, Nuremburg, Germany, dating from c1895. This spirit-fired steam locomotive, in tinplate with a brass boiler and fittings, is of the type popularly known as "Storklegs", a somewhat obscure expression, probably of American origin, referring to its wheel arrangement. The front pairs of wheels are not on a bogie, as the photograph may suggest, but are fixed. Note such detail as the dummy front lamps and the whistle protruding through the cab roof. The locomotive is 15in (38·1cm) long overall and has a maximum height of 8·5in (21·59cm). This example featured in the very popular movie "The Railway Children" (1970), in which it "blew up" in a spectacular manner—a real possibility if the safety-valve (on the boiler nearest the cab in the photograph) should malfunction. It may be noted that it is possible to find coal-fired locomotives of this type, but these are generally custom-made models and are hardly to be described as toys. The locomotive was offered at £2 10s 0d (£2.50, $3.00) in the 1902 Catalogue of A.W. Gamage, London; a high price in those days. Like all Gauge "4" items by Bing, it is now rare.

2 "3¾" Gauge—but built approximately to ¾in: 1ft (1·9cm: 30·5cm) scale—2-4-0 Locomotive by J. Bateman & Co., Great Britain, dating from c1880 and based on a London and North-Western Railway locomotive of the period. It is shown as obtained by the author, without tender, and has a length of 18in (45·72cm). It has no cab, simply a "spectacle plate" as was usual in British locomotives of the time, and is a most sophisticated model, with full boiler fittings, including a Salter-type safety-valve, regulator, pressure-gauge, water-gauge, and reversing gear. A spirit-fired steam model (spirit carried in tender and fed through a drip-feed) it works to high pressure, about 45 p.s.i., and was probably intended for a "garden railway", although in the enormous houses that were favoured by the well-to-do of the Victorian and Edwardian eras, such a model might well have been run indoors. In good working order, this engine would be quite capable, with its six-wheeled tender, of hauling some 12 pieces of rolling stock (which at that time were often made of polished mahogany). Bateman's model-making firm was established in 1774, and in the 19th century operated as the "Original Model Dockyard".

3 An attractive 2-2-2 "Piddler" or "Dribbler"—so called from their propensity to leave in their wake a trail of moisture from their cylinders—dating from c1880 and catalogued and advertised in Great Britain by Clyde Model Dockyard (basically a retailer rather than a maker). In spirit-fired steam (externally fired, with steam exhausting through the chimney), this is a fairly superior example for its time in that it has

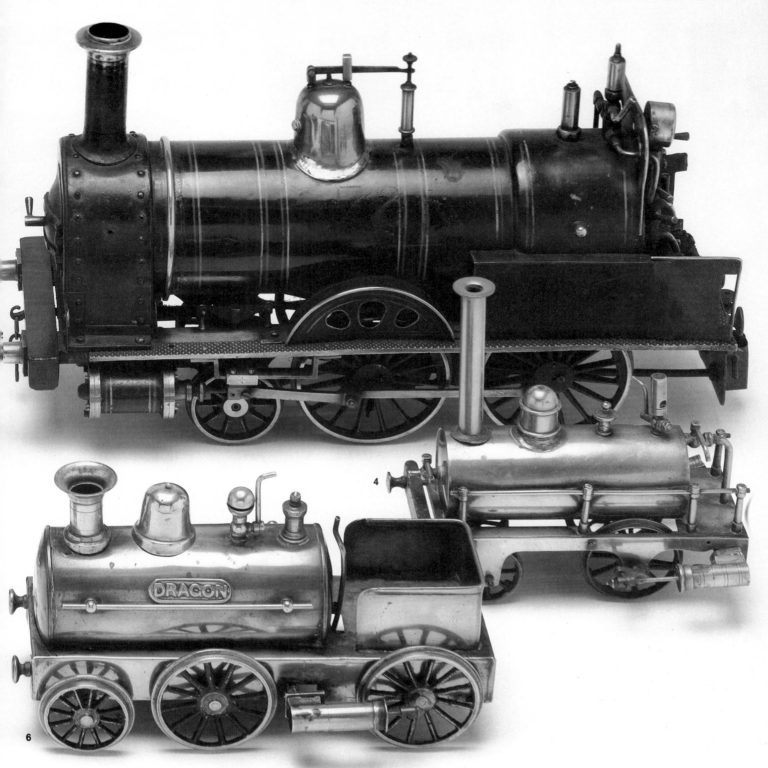

slide-valve cylinders. The pressure dome and whistle are missing, but note the regulator and water-level cock above the footplate. With a length of 10in (25·4cm), it is not built to scale: its wheels are pre-set to run on curved track of 3in (7·62cm) width, and it was most likely sold with a circle of track but with no provision for a tender or rolling stock. "Piddlers" were much favoured by collectors in the 1960s, when examples like this might sell for around £150.00 ($180.00): in the 1970s prices fell sharply, but they are now once again becoming popular.

4 A small all-brass "Piddler" by Newton & Co., Great Britain, a scientific instrument maker noted for "Piddlers" of all sizes, of superior workmanship and finish. Note the range of boiler fittings and the wooden buffer beam on this example, the latter a mark of the good-quality "Piddler", and the water-level cock on the front of the firebox. Of archaic appearance, almost "Rocket"-like, it in fact dates from c1880. A spirit-fired steam locomotive (externally fired, with oscillating cylinders) it is not intended to pull rolling stock, simply to run around a circular track. This example is in "2⅛" (5·4cm) Gauge—there were, of course, no standard gauges at the time of manufacture—and is 7in (17·78cm) long, with a height of 7·5in (19·05cm) to the top of its high funnel.

5 "2¾" Gauge 4-2-2 Locomotive by Stevens Model Dockyard, Great Britain, dating from c1890: a somewhat simplified but nevertheless recognisable representation of a Great Northern Railway "Single" (ie, with a large single driving wheel) of the period. It has a copper boiler, which was probably originally painted, and brass fittings. A spirit-fired steam model with slide-valve cylinders, it is semi-internally fired. This example, 12in (30·48cm) long, has undergone some restoration; but note that there was apparently never any provision for couplings.

6 "Dragon", a most attractive 2-2-2 "Piddler" of copper and brass. It is believed by the author to be the work of Radiguet et Massiot, France, a scientific instrument maker famous for stationary steam engines and toy boats, and was marketed in Britain in the 1880s by Clyde Model Dockyard. Spirit-fired, with oscillating cylinders, it is, like (4), of archaic appearance for its time and has no provision for couplings. Note the whistle and safety-valve (at rear of boiler): identical fittings are found on locomotives by various makers of the period and were probably standard parts made on the continent and imported to Britain. Like many "Piddlers", especially those of Clyde and Stevens Model Dockyards, this locomotive was available either ready-made or in kit form: kits were sold as early as the 1870s. This example is 9·5in (24·13cm) long.

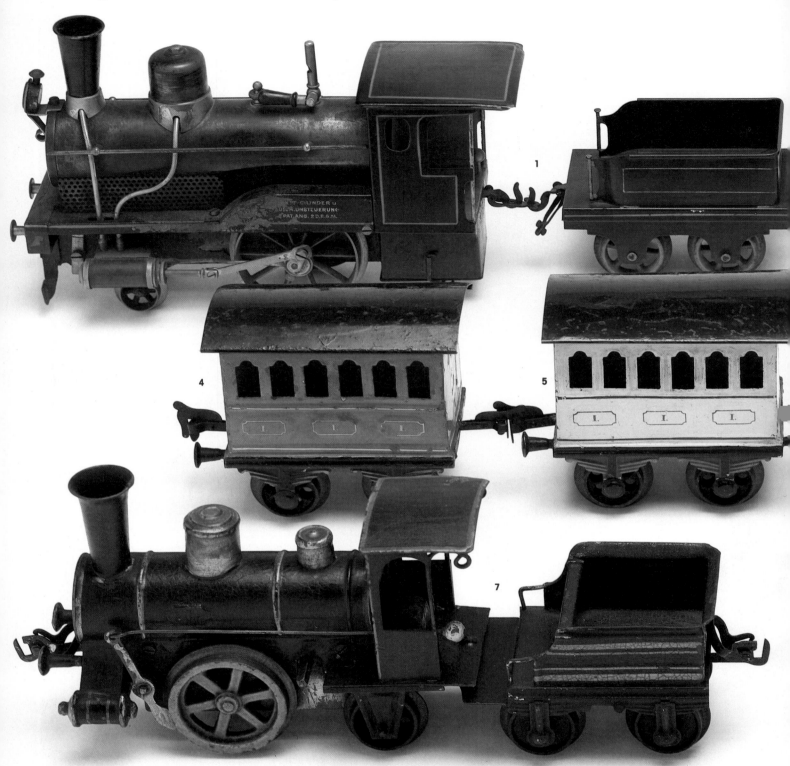

1-3 Gauge "2" Locomotive and Four-Wheeled Tender (1), with rolling stock (2-3), by Gebrüder Bing, Nuremburg, Germany. The locomotive is basically another version of the Gauge "4" 4-2-0 locomotive shown at (1) on *pages 36-37*. However, this smaller locomotive — the overall length of engine and tender is 15in (38·1 cm) — has a 2-2-0 wheel arrangement, one pair of leading wheels being thought sufficient by the maker. It can be dated with some certainty to around the same time as the larger locomotive, c1895, since it was found in Sydney, Australia, in the shop of an optician who had received it as a Christmas present when a child, in 1897. Its elderly owner kindly let it go to

the author's "good home", along with six pieces of rolling stock, for a nominal sum — although such items are rare and are generally expensive. The locomotive is tinplate, with an oxidized brass boiler and cast-iron wheels; a spirit-fired steam model, it has the familiar Bing slide-valve cylinders and the usual boiler fittings — pressure dome, safety-valve, and whistle — and is fitted with reversing gear. Note the dummy lamp in front of the chimney (such features are often missing from specimens of this vintage) and the German patent information, now partly obliterated, stamped on the side of the cab. The four-wheeled tender is of the type standard for Bing locomotives of the time.

At the time of manufacture, this item would have been marketed as a boxed set, along with three wagons (or two wagons and a passenger coach) and a circle of track. It is shown here with two pieces of its original rolling stock: a four-wheeled Cattle Truck (2), and a four-wheeled Brake/Goods Wagon (3) with sliding doors at the centre and an attractive and interesting "guard's look-out" cabin, complete with access ladder, at the rear. It is interesting also to note that both wagons are certainly Gauge "1" items that were fitted by Bing with Gauge "2" wheels for sale with the Gauge "2" locomotive. As was usual at this period, all the elements of the set are hand-painted.

4-6 Gauge "1" 0-2-2 Locomotive and Four-Wheeled Tender (6), clockwork-powered, with rolling stock (4-5), by Bing. This particular locomotive has caused considerable interest among collectors: no other example fitted with connecting-rods, as seen here, has yet been found; nor does the locomotive appear ever to have been catalogued in this form. Clockwork locomotives of this period do not usually have connecting-rods — see the typical Märklin engine at (7) — but there is no doubt that these are original fittings: they were certainly not added at a later date. The item can be fairly precisely dated from its most distinctive buffers and couplings, quite unlike those used by Bing at other

times, which the author's researches show to have been fitted only in 1895-97. The powerful clockwork motor, a simple non-reversing mechanism, has all-brass gears giving two "speeds": "Stop" and "Very Fast"! Rim-operating brakes, as seen acting on the large driving wheels, were fitted by both Bing and Märklin at this time. The locomotive is of tinplate with nickel-plated domes and connecting-rods: although the nickel here is in good condition, it may corrode, but it remained in use until the introduction of chrome-plating in the 1920s. Unusually, this example bears no trademark other than the raised "GB" (Gebrüder Bing)— on the boiler side. The overall

length of engine and tender is 13in (33·02cm). The attractive hand-painted Passenger Coaches (4-5) are typical of the period: the shape of their windows provides another dating feature. When sold as a set, with a circle of track, three coaches would have been provided. Like all pre-1900 items, this is rare.

7 Gauge "1" 0-2-2 Locomotive and Four-Wheeled Tender by Gebrüder Märklin, Germany, dating from c1895. It is interesting to compare this clockwork locomotive with that at (6) by Bing, Märklin's great Nuremburg rival. Most collectors seem to believe—although the author does not necessarily agree—that Märklin items of this kind are more desirable than those of

Bing: at any rate, Märklin pieces consistently fetch higher prices at auction. On this tinplate engine, hand-painted with gold-painted domes, note particularly how the coupling of the tender differs from the Bing example: the "stepped" arrangement is a typical Märklin feature. It has a simple non-reversing clockwork mechanism with brass gears and no speed governor. The silver-coloured knob of the brake lever for the rim-brake acting on both sides protrudes from the rear of the cab. A plaque on the boiler, just visible in the photograph, bears the raised figure "1", signifying the gauge. Overall length of engine and tender is 11in (27·94cm).

8 Gauge "1" 0-4-0 Locomotive

and Four-Wheeled Tender, clockwork, by Märklin. This is the same size as the Märklin locomotive at (7) but dates a little later, c1898. Again it is hand-painted and has a Gauge "1" mark on the boiler. However, the gears of the clockwork mechanism are a mixture of brass and steel and, like the Bing example at (6), it has nickel-plated domes: both steel gears and nickel-plating were probably just coming into use at this period. Like the other locomotives on this spread it has spoked wheels, but note that those on the tender have drilled holes. The Märklin trademark of the period—a shield enclosing the letters "GM"—is embossed on the front of the boiler.

All the trains shown on this spread are the property of the author, Ron McCrindell, and are currently on loan to the London Toy and Model Museum, October House, 21/23 Craven Hill, London W2, where they were photographed.

1 Gauge "1" PLM Pacific 2-3-1 Locomotive and Eight-Wheeled Tender by Gebrüder Märklin, Göppingen, Germany. (Note that 2-3-1 is the continental designation for a Pacific locomotive, as opposed to the British and US usage, 4-6-2.) This magnificent tinplate locomotive, clockwork-driven in the case of the example shown here, and a rare and much sought-after collector's item, was first made by Märklin in 1912 and remained available, in steam—see

(1), *pages 68-69*—and electric-driven versions also, for some years. It was still in the maker's catalogue, in electric only, as late as 1930. The locomotive shown here dates from around 1920 and is fitted with Märklin's standard, powerful, six-coupled geared-wind mechanism. Thus driven, it runs very well, unlike the steam version which, like most steam-driven locomotives by Märklin, is much too heavy because of the many castings used in its construction. (Märklin did not make a really satisfactory steam-driven locomotive until its final steam model—a Deutschbahn Pacific made in Gauges "0" and "1". This appeared in 1936 and was made only until 1939, it is, consequently, now very rare). A particular point of interest

on the locomotive shown is the retailer's plate on the side of the cab, indicating that it was supplied by Märklin to "Au Paradis des Enfants", a famous toyshop in Paris, France. This locomotive is modelled on the famous "231A Class" of the Paris-Lyon-Mediterranée (PLM) Railway. These were express engines especially celebrated for their fine performance when hauling the romantically evocative "Blue Train" on the Paris-Monte Carlo run, and they were among the few railway engines to be immortalized in music by a composer of note: Honegger's wonderfully descriptive composition "Pacific 231" vividly recalls the atmosphere of these remarkable locomotives. Some collectors will, perhaps, recall with pleasure a fine

colour-documentary movie issued in the late 1950s which, without spoken commentary, blended Honegger's music with action shots of a PLM Pacific. Length (engine and tender); 27·5in (69·85cm).

2 Gauge "1" "Mitropa" Sleeping Car by Märklin; a very handsome item from the maker's 1920 Series, in tinplate and virtually hand-made, with all joints soldered—no tongue-and-slot construction here! It is hand-painted in simulated wood finish and runs on cast bogies with steel wheels. Interior fittings include beds with reclining plaster figures (peacefully sleeping—not, as in the case of Märklin's sitting passengers, noted on other spreads, impaled on spikes!). Like the PLM Pacific locomotive with which

it is shown, this is a rare and valuable item. Length: 20·866in (53cm).

3-4"3¼in" Gauge 4-2-2 Locomotive, "Zulu", and Six-Wheeled Tender (3), shown here with an Open Wagon (4), made by Shaw of London, an optical instrument maker. A brass plate on the side of the cab bears the maker's name and the date "1891": it is rare to be able to identify such a model so precisely. This is a good example of the kind of model then being produced to order by the optical instrument makers concentrated in London's West End and, as is usually the case, is of rather archaic appearance (but delightfully so) for its date of manufacture. The copper boiler is spirit-fired and the locomotive has an impressive array of fittings, included cab-operated

Stephenson's link-gear reversing, lever-type regulator, water gauge, pressure gauge, whistle, displacement lubricator, level cocks, and lever safety-valve. The locomotive's wheels are sprung, as are those of the attractive tender, which houses a spirit reservoir. The period wagon is constructed of mahogany, with all brass fittings and leaf springing. Lengths (engine and tender): 25in (63·5cm); (wagon): 13in (33·02cm).

5 Gauge "1" Great Northern "Single" 4-2-2 Locomotive, numbered "266", and Six-Wheeled Tender, made by Gebrüder Bing, Nuremburg, Germany, for Bassett-Lowke, Great Britain, and dating from about 1910. This clockwork-driven model is a good representation of the Ivatt Singles that replaced the Stirling 8-Footers in light, fast passenger

service on the Great Northern Railway. It is typical of the fine true-to-prototype models made by Bing for Bassett-Lowke up to 1914: only a few comparable items appeared after World War I. Well-finished and hand-painted, it has a two-speed mechanism that would, Bassett-Lowke claimed, give a run of over 200ft (60m) on one winding. It was priced in the UK at £3 10s 0d (£3.50, $4.20) in 1911; a very considerable sum for that time. Length (engine and tender): 20in (50·8cm).

6 Gauge "1" London and North-Western Railway (L&NWR) "Cauliflower" 0-6-0 Locomotive, numbered "930", and Six-Wheeled Tender; like (5), this was made by Bing for Bassett-Lowke around 1910, and is fitted with a two-speed

clockwork mechanism. It is modelled on the six-coupled engines designed by Webb for the L&NWR as fast goods locomotives; these were so successful that they were frequently used on passenger services. The L&NWR crest that in real practice featured prominently on the centre driving-wheel splashers of these locomotives (although it is not to be seen on this model) looked, at a distance, like the familiar vegetable—hence, the engines were called "Cauliflowers", a nickname that remained with them all their days and is still used by railway enthusiasts. This model was also available from Bassett-Lowke in less authentic Midland Railway livery, in that case numbered "3044". Length (engine and tender): 18in (45·72cm).

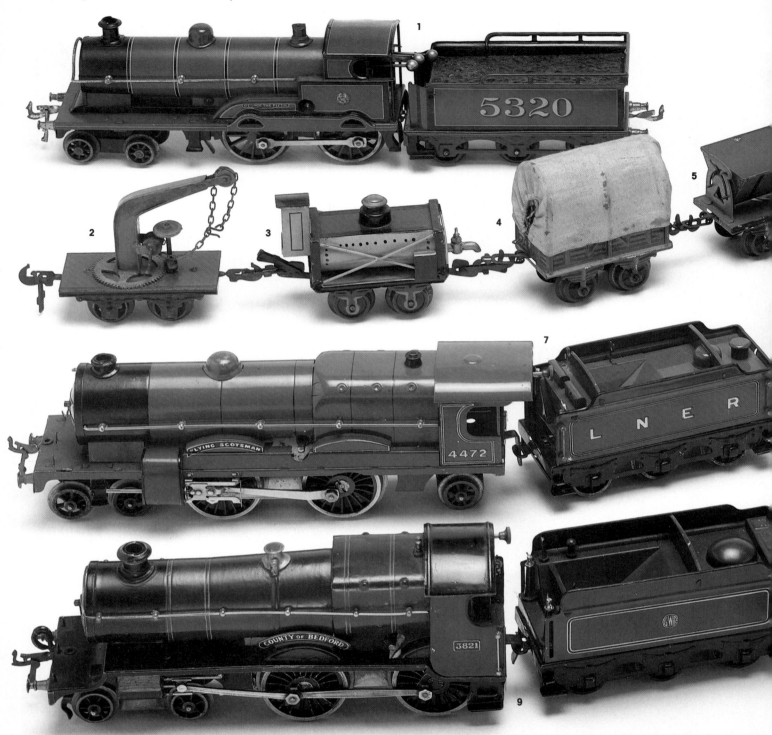

1 Gauge "0" "George the Fifth" Locomotive and Six-Wheeled Tender, numbered "5320", made by Gebrüder Bing, Nuremburg, Germany, for sale in Great Britain by Bassett-Lowke. This example dates from the mid-1920s, but the model was available as early as 1912 and was made in quantity until well into the 1920s. Originally available in black, with the correct number of the prototype, "2663"—see (7-8), *pages 54-55*—it subsequently appeared in several different liveries—the example shown is in London, Midland & Scottish Railway (LMS) colours—and with different names, including "Minerva" and "Queen Mary". It was made in Gauges "0", "1", and "2" (available only in black in

the two larger gauges) and in clockwork, as seen here, and electric: a "de luxe" version with generally superior finish and with better-scaled wheels was available in Gauge "0". It is a most attractive item and, because of its long production run, not too difficult to find. Length (engine and tender): 16in (40·64cm).

2-6 Gauge "0" Steam Train; an early train, dating from around 1895 and featuring models of that period by three great German makers. The simple 0-4-0 Locomotive (6) in spirit-fired steam, with a single cylinder inside the cab and an exterior flywheel, is by Bing, and was catalogued in 1895 at a price of 4s 6d (22½p, 27c). In spite of its age it is in excellent working

order and is regularly run on the author's layout. Length: 6in (15·24cm). The Hopper Wagon (5), with tipping action, and Covered Wagon (4), with a tarpaulin held by a draw-string, are both by Bing; both are 3·5in (8·99cm) long. The Water Wagon (3), with its rear-mounted guard's (look-out) compartment, can be filled through the cap on top and emptied through its tap; made by Märklin, it was also sold as a Tar Wagon. It is 4·75in (12·06cm) long. The Crane Truck (2), with a working, rotatable crane, is by Carette, and is 3·5in (8·89cm) long. All these items are handpainted.

7 Gauge "0" "Flying Scotsman" 4-4-2 Locomotive, numbered "4472", and Six-Wheeled Tender,

made by Hornby, Great Britain; this model had a long production run, from *c*1928 until 1940. Although the number is that of the real "Flying Scotsman", neither the outline nor the wheel arrangement bear much resemblance to the prototype, which was a Pacific (4-6-2). However, the 4-4-2 arrangement does improve the model's negotiation of sharp curves on the track. Produced as part of Hornby's "No 3 Locomotive Series", which also included "Royal Scot", the model was available in clockwork, as shown, with an excellent long-running mechanism, or electric. Seen here in London and North Eastern Railway (LNER) livery, it was made also in other major

liveries and other names; the tender is the standard one for the series. Length (engine and tender): 16in (40·64cm). A famous model, this is one of the easier Hornby items for collectors to acquire—although it may prove to be expensive.

8 Gauge "0" "Alberta" Hornby No 2 Special Composite Coach, in the Pullman livery of the late 1920s. This bogie coach features opening end and luggage compartment doors, celluloid windows with printed details of lamps, and provision for corridor connections. It was available with other names: "Alberta" is believed to be one of the rarer examples. Length: 13in (33·02cm). See also (10-11).

9 Gauge "0" "County of Bedford" 4-4-0 Locomotive, numbered

"3821", and Six-Wheeled Tender, made by Hornby, Great Britain. This model was an early item in Hornby's "No 2 Special" series, introduced in late 1929. It represented an important advance by Hornby: for the first time, almost true-to-prototype models were produced, beginning with this example in authentic Great Western Railway (GWR) outline, and at later dates including an LMS Midland Compound, Southern Railway (SR) L.1. Class, LNER "Yorkshire" and "Bramham Moor", and SR Schools Class "Eton". All were 4-4-0 locomotives with either four-coupled clockwork mechanism, as shown, or electric. The series proved very popular and its authenticity did much to enhance the appearance

of model railways. The loco- motives were available separately or could be purchased in a boxed set with track and, usually, two Pullman cars, at a price in the early 1930s of £3 5s 0d (£3.25, $3.90) in clockwork or £3 15s 0d (£3.75, $4.50) in electric. Length (engine and tender): 15·25in (38·73cm).

10-11 Gauge "0" Bogie Pullman Cars, "Iolanthe" and "Montana" (the latter one of the rarer names) in the later Pullman livery— compare with (8)—as they appeared from Hornby from the mid-1930s until 1940. Save for lithography and roof colour, they are identical with (8).

12 Gauge "0" 4-4-0 Locomotive, numbered "142", and Eight- Wheeled (two bogies) Tender,

made by Bing for Bassett-Lowke. In Caledonian Railway blue livery, and based on the famous "140 Class' Dunalastaires of the CR, this was felt by Bassett-Lowke to be one of its most realistic models, and it is, indeed, a most attractive and desirable item. First appearing in 1914, it remained in Bassett-Lowke's Catalogue as late as 1927, initially available, as seen here, in clockwork only, but during the 1920s in electric also. The original price of £2 2s 0d (£2.10, $2.52) had risen to £4 4s 0d (£4.20, $5.04) by 1927. It was made in Gauges "0" and "1" and, while now very difficult to find in any gauge, it is, as is usual, rarer in Gauge "0" than in "1". Length (engine and tender): 16in (40·64cm).

1 Gauge "1" tinplate Private Owner's Wagon, lettered "W. J. Bassett-Lowke & Co", made by Carette, Nuremburg, Germany, for sale in Great Britain by Bassett-Lowke. It is one of the models of the 1909 series, which continued to appear up to 1914, and, like the other items from the series shown on this spread, was available in Gauges "0", "1", and "2"; the original prices given are those for the gauges shown. This example has been well-used and the lithographed lettering is somewhat faded, but it is still possible to read the slogan "Deal Direct With Manufacturers"—as noted earlier, Bassett-Lowke liked to give the impression that the models it marketed were British-made—along with the address of the firm's London retail outlet. This wagon was offered in Bassett-Lowke's 1911 Catalogue at a price of 3s 6d (17½p, 21c). Although it cannot be seen in the photograph, the wagon bears on its sole plate the number "809", which may be taken to refer to the date of the model: August 1909. Length: 7·25in (18·41cm).

2 Gauge "1" tinplate Refrigerator Meat Van, in Midland Railway livery and numbered "7803", made by Gebrüder Märklin, Germany, for sale in Britain by A. W. Gamage, London, and dating from 1909. It was offered in Gamage's 1911 Catalogue at a price of 2s 11d (14¼p, 17c). Length: 7·25in (18·41cm).

3 Gauge "1" tinplate Mica B Refrigerator Meat Van, in Great Western Railway livery and numbered "39761", made by Carette, 1909 series, for Bassett-Lowke, by whom it was catalogued in 1911 at 3s 6d (17½p, 21c). Length: 7·25in (18·41cm).

4 Gauge "1" tinplate Motor Car Traffic Van, in London and North Western Railway (L&NWR) livery, made by Carette for Bassett-Lowke, 1909 series. This was based on a prototype used by Mulliner's, a famous coach-building firm, to transport Rolls Royce automobiles. It was priced at 4s 0d (20p, 24c) in Bassett-Lowke's 1911 Catalogue. Length: 9·5in (24·13cm).

5 Gauge "1" tinplate Open Wagon, lettered "City of Birmingham Gas Dept", "Saltley Works", "No 1201", made by Carette for Bassett-Lowke, 1909 series, and priced at 3s 6d (17½p, 21c) in 1911. Length: 7in (11·78cm).

6 Gauge "1" tinplate Open Wagon, the same model as (5), but lettered "W. H. Hull & Son", "Birmingham", and numbered "405", made by Carette for Bassett-Lowke, 1909 series. Catalogue price and length are as (5).

7 Gauge "1" tinplate Cement Wagon, lettered "Greaves Blue Lias Lime" and "Greaves Portland Cement", "Harbury", and numbered "130", made by Carette for Bassett-Lowke, 1909 series. This attractive model in the

livery of the East Wiltshire Joint Railway (EWJR) has a tarpaulin over its central loading aperture. It was priced at 4s 0d (20p, 24c) in Bassett-Lowke's 1911 Catalogue. Length 7in (17·78cm).

8 Gauge "1" tinplate Tarpaulin-Covered Wagon of the London, Brighton and South Coast Railway (LB&SCR), made by Carette for Bassett-Lowke, 1909 series. Bassett-Lowke's "Lowko" trademark and the number "1911", which may be taken as the date of this example, appear on the sole plate. It was priced at 4s 0d (20p, 24c) in Bassett-Lowke's 1911 Catalogue. Length: 7in (17·78cm).

9-10 Gauge "4" Wagons: a pair of beautifully hand-enamelled tinplate wagons made by Bing in c1895

for sale in Britain by Gamage's, and priced in the 1902 Catalogue at 5s 6d (27½p, 33c) each. These wagons were made to run with the 4-2-0 locomotive shown at (1) on *pages 36-37*. Length: 8·25in (20·95cm).

11 Gauge "2" Bogie Wagon by Bing; a most attractive hand-enamelled tinplate wagon in continental style from an early series, dating from the early 1900s. It has two opening doors on each side. Available in Gauges "0", "1", "2", and "3", it was marketed in Britain by Gamage's and was priced at 3s 9d (19p, 23c) in c1905. Length: 14·5in (36·83cm).

12 Gauge "1" tinplate Petrol Tank Wagon by Bing, dating from c1905. This diminutive

model bears on the end the legend "Petroleum Comp": the screw-top can be opened to enable a juvenile owner to fill it with liquid — hopefully with water rather than petrol! This model appeared in Gamage's Catalogue, c1905, at a price of 1s 11d (9½p, 11c) in Gauge "1", or 1s 3d (6½p, 8c) in Gauge "0". Length: 5·25in (13·3cm).

13 Gauge "1" tinplate Private Owner's Wagon; like (1), this is lettered "Bassett-Lowke, Northampton", but it is from a later series than the other Carette wagons shown on this spread. This was, in fact, made in Britain for Bassett-Lowke during the 1920s, using Carette pressings acquired after World War I (the French-owned firm having ceased production in 1917).

This example was completely overpainted in black, traces of which remain, when the author obtained it. Length: 7in (17·78cm).

14 Gauge "1" tinplate Tar Wagon, made by Carette for Bassett-Lowke, 1909 series. Like some other wagons of the series it bears the number "1909", which it is safe to take as a date. This is a fairly rare model. It was priced at 3s 6d (17½p, 21c) in Bassett-Lowke's 1911 Catalogue. Length: 7in (17·78cm).

15 Gauge "1" tinplate 15-Ton Wagon, in Great Northern Railway livery and numbered "2821", made by Märklin for Gamage's and dating from c1910. It was priced at 2s 6d (12½p, 15c) in Gamage's 1911 Catalogue. Length: 8·5in (21·59cm).

1 Gauge "1" 4-4-0 Locomotive and Six-Wheeled Tender made by Gebrüder Bing, Nuremberg, Germany, for sale in Britain by Bassett-Lowke Limited, Northampton, who first catalogued this item in 1903. The example shown is in Midland Railway livery: it was also available in the liveries of the London and North-Western Railway (L&NWR), Great Northern Railway (GNR), and London and South-Western Railway (L&SWR). When obtained by the author it was completely over-painted and, as seen now, is the result of many hours of painstaking restoration. In tinplate with brass domes, it is fitted with a two-speed clockwork mechanism: protruding from the cab are the speed regulator

(fast/slow), and forward and reverse levers. The number "2631" on the tender was used by Bing up to 1914 on a long series of locomotives in Midland livery. The overall length of the locomotive and tender is 19in (48·26cm).

2 Gauge "1" 2-2-2 "Lady of the Lake" Locomotive, numbered "531", made in 1902 by Carette, Nuremburg, Germany, for sale in Britain by Bassett-Lowke — at an original price of £1 11s 0d (£1·55, $1·86) in Gauge "1" or £1 13s 6d (£1.67½, $2.01) in Gauge "2". It is interesting to note that this locomotive was one of the very first commercially-made models to bear a good likeness to its prototype; ie, the real locomotive on which it was

based. "Lady of the Lake" was a famous locomotive of the L&NWR, whose livery it wears, as early as the 1850s; thus, the style of the model is much earlier than its date of manufacture. A spirit-fired steam engine with twin oscillating cylinders (partly concealed by the cylinder casings, in order to give a more realistic appearance when running), it is fitted with the spoked wheels of superior quality that were made available by Bassett-Lowke at a slight extra charge. Note that the leading pair of wheels is mounted on a pony truck (ie, with two pivoted wheels; a bogie has four pivoted wheels) to enable the locomotive to negotiate tight curves on the track. This is an extremely rare item: the

author knows of only four extant examples, of which two (including the example shown, which is seen with a six-wheeled tender by Bing, dating from c1909) do not have the original Carette tender. The overall length of locomotive and tender is 19in (48·26cm).

3-4 Gauge "11" Corridor Car (3) and Dining Car (4) by Märklin, Germany, dating from 1903. These attractively hand-painted tinplate coaches are of somewhat continental appearance: they were marketed by Märklin in Europe in German, French and Swiss railway colours; a Hospital Coach version, with a large red cross on the side, was produced for the continental market, and they were also exported, with appropriate

decoration, to the USA. They were made in all four gauges—"0", "1", "2", "3"—then advertised by Märklin. The version seen here is in L&NWR livery, as supplied for sale in Britain by the famous department store of A. W. Gamage, London. The original price of the corridor car (both were also available in Midland Railway livery) was 10s 6d (52½p, 63c). Both coaches have opening doors and roofs that open on hinges to reveal such detail as: (3), an end lavatory with wash-basin and commode, baggage racks, and seats with spikes on which the terracotta passengers are securely—and seemingly contentedly!—impaled; and (4), tables and seats, with an end kitchen. These coaches,

each 11in (27·94cm) long, are hard to find.

5 Gauge "1" Express Bogie Coach, made by Märklin for sale in Britain by Gamage, 1903, and available also in Gauges "0", "2", and "3". Made of tinplate and hand-painted in Midland Railway livery (it was also available in L&NWR colours), it has opening doors with cast-metal handles, a slide-off roof and, like (3), seats with spikes to accommodate the unfortunate passengers! Note the "steps" at the coach's end, in reality intended to give the conductor access to the roof with its lamp tops. The coach is 12in (30·48cm) long. The legend "Made in Germany" is stamped on its underside, but it bears no Märklin trademark,

which appears irregularly on items of this period. Also unseen in the photograph is an applied plaque with the embossed "Gamage" mark on the coach's end—a most desirable feature for the collector. A rare item.

6-7 Gauge "1" 4-4-0 Locomotive, numbered "593", and Six-Wheeled Tender, with Four-Wheeled Passenger Coach (Third Class), made by Bing for sale in Britain by Basset-Lowke in 1903 —in the same series as the locomotive shown at (1) above. This locomotive and its attractively-lithographed tinplate coach, with the addition of a Brake Van and an oval of track, formed part of a set that was offered by Bassett-Lowke at a price of £1 15s 0d (£1·75, $2·10) in Gauge

"1", or £1 5s 6d (£1·27½, $1·53) in Gauge "0". It was also available in Gauge "2", and could be had in the liveries of the L&SWR, as shown here, L&NWR, Midland Railway, and Great Northern Railway. The coach has non-opening doors. At about the time of manufacture of this item, Bing was introducing a more powerful clockwork mechanism. Note, therefore, that in this example the winding shaft is on the right hand side, whereas in (1) it is on the left: this dates (1) as the later item, probably by a few months, with a more powerful mechanism and heavier wheels. The overall length of the engine and tender is 20in (50·8cm); length of coach: 9·5in (24·13cm).

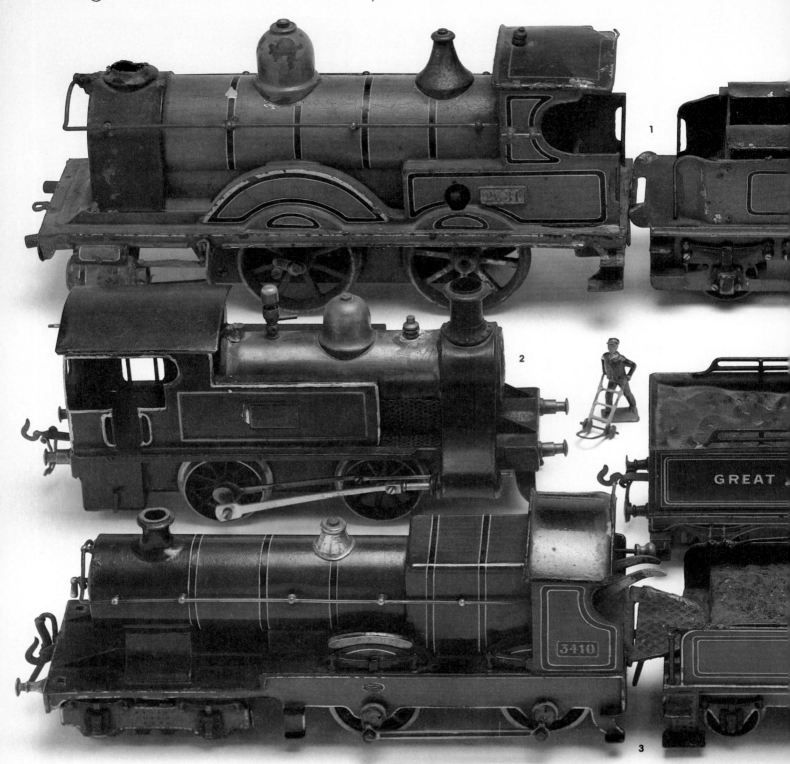

1 Gauge "3" 0-4-0 Locomotive, numbered "2631" on an applied plate on the cab, and Six-Wheeled Tender, made by Gebrüder Bing, Nuremburg, Germany, and dating—on the evidence of the winding shaft on the left hand side—from c1903. Note that the number is the same as that of the Gauge "1" Bing locomotive of the same period shown at (1) on *pages 46-47*. Inside the cab is a Bing trademark of the period: this indicates that the locomotive was made for sale in Great Britain by A. W. Gamage, since Bassett-Lowke preferred to give the impression that the toys it marketed were British-made, and was careful to see that Bing's trademarks did not appear on its products.

This locomotive was available in both clockwork, as shown, and steam models, and in Gauges "3" and "4" only. (It is worth noting at this point that Gauge "4" models run on 3in (7·62cm) track; Gauge "3" on 2·5in (6·35cm) track; and only Gauge "2" on 2in (5·08cm) track as the designation implies.) Gamage's price for this item in the 1903 Catalogue was £2 15s 0d (£2.75, $3.30) in Gauge "3", or £3 3s 0d (£3·15, $3·78) in Gauge "4". This particular example is in well "played-with" condition, with its smokestack and connecting-rods missing, and needs restoration—which would be well worthwhile, since it is a comparatively rare item. It is in Midland Railway livery; it was

available in Britain also in L&NWR livery and, on the continent, in the colours of various European railroads. Gauge "3" and "4" engines were the largest commercially-made trains in which clockwork was employed, and the massive mechanism of this locomotive —two-speed, with forward and reverse gears—takes all an adult's strength to wind. The overall length of engine and tender is 23·6in (60cm).

2 Gauge "1" 0-4-0 Tank Engine by Bing, dating from c1902; a fairly accurate representation of a North London Railway tank locomotive of the period, produced to follow the maker's more celebrated Gauge "2" version of 1901. A spirit-fired

steam model, this has a single oscillating cylinder in the cab and, as the author has found over a 20-year period, runs well and is surprisingly powerful for a single-cylinder locomotive. Made of tinplate, it has a brass boiler and fittings and is 11in (27·94cm) long. This locomotive was sold in Britain by both Bassett-Lowke and Gamage, the latter cataloguing it at a price of 14s 9d (73½p, 88c) in Gauge "1", or 9s 9d (48½p, 58c) in Gauge "0".

3 Gauge "1" "Sydney" 4-4-0 Locomotive, numbered "3410", and Six-Wheeled Tender, made by Bing, c1905, for sale in Britain by Bassett-Lowke. This is a clockwork model with a two-speed mechanism, with

forward and reverse gears, an automatic brake, and, in the words of Bassett-Lowke's catalogue, "patent governors to prevent derailing when running light". A similar model to the GWR's famous "City of Truro" locomotive, this is attractive and well detailed: note the engine's brass dome and handrail, and the pressed-tin "coal" top of the tender. It was available in Gauges "0", "1", and "2"—at prices of £1 1s 0d (£1·05, $1·26), £2 2s 0d (£2·10, $2·52), and £3 7s 6d (£3·37½, $4·05) respectively—but only, as shown, in the livery of the Great Western Railway (GWR). The overall length of engine and tender is 20in (50·8cm).

4 Gauge "1" "Sir Alexander" 4-4-0 Bogie Express Locomotive,

numbered "1014", and Six-Wheeled Tender, made by Bing in 1903, for sale in Britain by Bassett-Lowke. This was described by Bassett-Lowke as the firm's first scale-model locomotive—"an official working model in ⅜in scale"—and although not precisely to scale it is, indeed, very accurate for its period. Based on a Great Central Railway express locomotive of the time, it is finely enamelled—note particularly the "Great Central" crest on the tender—and well detailed: note the dummy vacuum hose brake pipe situated above the front buffers; and the steps forward of the front driving wheels, to the cab, and at either end of the tender. The two-speed clockwork

mechanism incorporates a patent governor, reversing gear, and automatic brake. The overall length of engine and tender is 20in (50·8cm). See (6) for a Coach made to match.

5 Gauge "1" Bogie Wagon by Märklin, Germany, dating from the early 1900s; marketed in Britain by Gamage and available in Gauges "0", "1", "2", "3", and "4". It is hand-painted and well detailed, with opening doors, as shown, on both sides, and steps at each end. Length: 8·5in (21·59cm).

6 Gauge "1" "Great Central Railway" Bogie Passenger Coach, made by Bing to match with the locomotive shown at (4). It has opening end doors and a slide-off roof (in this example,

a replacement item), but no interior detail. Although both are hard to find, this coach is somewhat rarer than the locomotive it complements. Length: 16in (40·64cm).

7 Gauge "2" Baggage Van, made by Märklin in c1902 for sale in Britain by Gamage, and originally priced at 4s 11d (25p, 30c). Hand-painted in Midland Railway livery, it was catalogued by Gamage in Gauges "2" and "3", and is known to have been available at various times in Gauges "0" and "1" also. It has the legend "Made in Germany" stamped on its underside and, at one end of its upper body, the applied white-metal "Gamage" plaque that is always a desirable addition. Length 10·5in (26·67cm).

1 Gauge "1" tinplate Bogie Passenger Coach by Gebrüder Bing, Nuremburg, Germany, dating from 1912. In continental railroad style, this coach was available in a plain version, as seen here, with a lithographed finish to simulate wood and without lettering, and also with the appropriate finish and lettering for a *Speisewagen* (Restaurant Car), *Schlafwagen* (Sleeping Car), and *Gepäckwagen* (Baggage Car). It was made in Gauges "0" and "1". The author believes that the plain version shown here was probably aimed at the US market, since it much resembles an American-style car. It has opening side doors at each end and the hinged roof lifts to show a detailed interior: a screen of black

cloth on a metal frame divides the compartments from the corridor; the seats are fitted with spikes to accommodate the figures of passengers; and at the end of the coach is a lavatory compartment complete with commode. A single dummy gas cylinder is fitted to the underside. Although this coach was first catalogued in 1912, and its style is of an earlier period, this particular example bears on its base a Bing trademark that indicates a date of manufacture after World War I. These continental coaches are not widely collected in the United Kingdom, although they may be found at swap-meets. Length: 13·5in (34·29cm).
2 Gauge "1" tinplate Restaurant Car by Bing, dating from 1912

and originally intended to make up part of a train pulled by the Bavarian State Railway 4-4-4 Locomotive shown at (1) on *pages 66-67*. This item is of particular interest in that it is the longest coach made by Bing: the Gauge "1" version shown here is 19·68in (50cm) long; it was made also in Gauge "0". These coaches were described as "Pullman Cars" in Bing's catalogue and, like (1), were available in various forms, lettered and non-lettered; it may well be that, like (1), this non-lettered example was again at least partly aimed at the American market. The hinged roof opens to show a detailed interior: a dining-car layout with chairs (with spikes for

passengers) and tables, and with kitchen fittings at each end. Provision is made for a cloth screen to mark the division between corridor and compartments. It has opening end doors and provision for corridor connections; dummy gas cylinders are fitted to the underside. These coaches remained in Bing's catalogue as late as 1927.
3 Gauge "1" tinplate Bogie Passenger Coach, First Class, numbered "132", made by Bing for sale in Great Britain by Bassett-Lowke; an item from what is known to collectors as the 1921 Series. These coaches were available in Gauges "0" and "1", and in the liveries of the London and North-Western Railway, see (6), and Midland Railway—and after 1923

the liveries of the LNER, LMS, SR and GWR. The example shown is in the "lake livery" (ie, crimson lake) which the GWR briefly adopted to replace its familiar "chocolate and cream". But soon after these coaches were made by Bing, the GWR reverted to "chocolate and cream" — which rather spoiled the sales of the "lake" examples. Bassett-Lowke therefore had many of these coaches over-painted by hand with other liveries, particularly that of Southern Railway, and catalogued and issued many of them as "Southern" coaches. For this reason, the coaches in their original livery are particularly popular with collectors. Note also that the coaches of this series, particularly the Gauge

"1" version, as shown, are over scale. The author believes that the series was, in fact, designed before World War I, when Gauge "2" was popular, and that Bassett-Lowke, failing to anticipate the trend towards Gauge "1", overstocked with Gauge "2" items. After World War I, however, Gauge "2" had completely fallen from favour, and thus Bassett-Lowke refitted the coaches with Gauge "1" wheels and issued them as Gauge "1" items. Nevertheless, they make up an effective train with Bassett-Lowke's Gauge "1" Mogul Locomotive, itself somewhat over scale. Opening doors are fitted, and the roof slides off to show a detailed interior: a tinplate screen divides the five separate compartments, with bench seats,

from the corridor. Dummy gas cylinders are fitted to the underside. Length: 18·5in (46·99cm).
4 Gauge "2" tinplate Guards Van made by Bing for Bassett-Lowke. This first appeared in Bassett-Lowke's 1902-03 Catalogue, where the Gauge "2" version was priced at £1 2s 6d (£1.12½, £1.35). A most attractive, early item, beautifully hand-painted, it was available in Gauges "1", "2", "3", and "4", and in the liveries of the Midland Railway, and, as seen here, London and South-Western Railway. It has opening double doors at each end and an opening single door centrally, on either side; the roof hinges open to reveal an interior divided into a central guard's (conductor's) compartment, with

tables and chairs, with opening interior doors to baggage compartments. Length: 10·75in (27·3cm). The guard at the window is a figure made by Britains, Great Britain, c1910.
5 Gauge "1" tinplate Four-Wheeled Passenger Coach, Third Class, made by Bing for Bassett-Lowke and catalogued as early as 1904. In London and South-Western Railway livery, it is an early example of lithography: most items of this period were hand-painted. Length: 9·5in (24·13cm).
6 Gauge "1" tinplate Bogie Passenger Coach, First Class, numbered "1921", made by Bing for Bassett-Lowke; like (3), a 1921 Series coach, and identical with (3) in all respects, but in L&NWR livery.

1 Gauge "1" tinplate Express Bogie Passenger Coach, First/Third Class, in Midland Railway livery and numbered "2873", made by Gebrüder Märklin, Germany, for sale in Great Britain by A.W. Gamage, London. Dating from c1910, this is an item from the series made by Märklin for Gamage's in direct competition with the similar coaches made by Carette, Nuremberg, Germany, for sale in Britain by Bassett-Lowke. It will be of interest to compare the Märklin/Gamage items shown here with their Carette/Bassett-Lowke equivalents shown on *pages 64-65;* as is shown elsewhere, the makers/retailers engaged in similar competition with series of freight rolling stock. Most items from the Märklin

series were available in Gauges "0" and "1". The coach shown here was made in two lengths: 12·5in (31·75cm) long, as seen here, in the form known by the author as a "bogie shorty"; and 16·5in (41·91cm) long, as shown at (6) on this spread. It was available with opening doors with cast metal handles, again as shown here, or with non-opening doors, as seen at (6). The roof slides off, but there is no interior detail. The legend "Germany" is stamped in orange on the underside. These coaches were made for Gamage in comparatively large numbers and are likely to be fairly easily found by collectors at swap-meets and elsewhere.
2 Gauge "1" tinplate Bogie Pullman

Car, named "Cleopatra", made by Märklin for the British market in c1928, and also available in Gauge "0". This coach — with three similar coaches respectively named "Alberta", "Dining Saloon", and "Car Number Four, Third Class" — was produced to run with Märklin's "Stephenson" Baltic (ie, with a 4-6-4 wheel arrangement) Tank Locomotive to make up a train resembling the famous British express "Southern Belle". The same items appeared briefly on the continent lettered "Golden Mountain Pullman Express", presumably aimed at the Swiss market: they were never sold in this form in Britain. The detail of the model is most pleasing — it has celluloid windows and is provided with

steps up to the opening doors — and it is unusual, for this relatively late period, in being hand-painted; the lettering and crests are part-transfer and part-handwork. The legend "Made in Germany", with a Märklin trademark, is stamped on the underside. These coaches appeared in the catalogues for only a short time and are believed to have been made in very limited numbers; thus, they are now rare, especially in Gauge "0", and command high prices. Length: 20in (50·6cm).
3 Gauge "1" tinplate Bogie Coach, First/Third Class, in London and North-Western Railway (L&NWR) livery and numbered "1153", made by Märklin for sale in Britain by Gamage's, c1910. The nicely lithographed coach is made up of

five passenger compartments (three Third Class; two First Class) and two lavatories; originally used by Carette in coaches made for Bassett-Lowke, this was established as Märklin's standard layout. It was available with opening doors as well as with non-opening doors, as shown here; the roof slides off, but there is no interior detail. Dummy gas cylinders—hardly visible here, but seen to better advantage on the Pullman at (2)—are fitted beneath it. The underside is stamped with the usual Märklin and Gamage marks of the period. This coach was priced at 5s 9d (28½p, 34c) in Gamage's 1913 Catalogue. Length: 16·5in (41·91cm).

4 Gauge "1" tinplate Dining Car by Märklin, dating from c1902.

This hand-painted bogie coach has already been noted at (4) on *pages 46-47,* where it is shown with Carette's contemporary "Lady of the Lake" locomotive; however, it makes an interesting comparison—with its hinged roof that opens to show considerable interior detail—with the later Märklin items shown here. Now a rare item, it was described in Gamage's 1902 Catalogue as a "Corridor Dining Car" and was priced then at 12s 6d (62½p, 75c) in Gauge "1"; it was available also in Gauges "0" and "2". Length: 11in (29·94cm).

5 Gauge "1" tinplate Four-Wheeled Suburban Coach ("Personen-wagen"), Third Class, in continental livery and numbered "18071", made by Märklin in c1930.

This coach was available in Gauges "0" and "1" until the outbreak of World War II; it appeared again briefly, in Gauge "0" only, in the late 1940s. It was made exclusively for the continental market and, although available in Britain on special order, is now rare in Britain. It is, of course, in continental style—note the observation platforms at the ends—and has opening connecting doors. The roof slides off, but there is no interior detail. Stuck to the underside is a paper label bearing instructions for lubricating the wheels. This coach is shown as part of a train at (2-4) on *pages 60-61.* The prototype of this coach was most unpopular with passengers because of poor springing and

excessive noise, and was given the nickname "Blunderbuss". Length: 10·5in (26·67cm).

6 Gauge "1" tinplate Express Bogie Passenger Coach, First/Third Class, in Midland Railway livery and numbered "2875", made by Märklin for Gamage's, c1910. This is the full-length version of the coach shown at (1), and also much resembles the L&NWR version shown at (3), although it is of better quality. Most attractively and colourfully lithographed, it has non-opening doors; the roof slides off, but there are no interior fittings. The dummy gas cylinders fitted beneath it are just visible in the photograph. This coach was priced at 7s 0d (35p, 42c) in Gamage's 1913 Catalogue. Length: 16·5in (41·91cm).

1-3 Gauge "0" 4-4-2 Locomotive, numbered "31801", and Eight-Wheeled (two bogies) Tender (3), with Sleeping Car (2) and Dining Car (1), by Hornby; the famous "Blue Train", so called from the colour of its coaches, modelled on the Calais-Mediterranean Express, and in the livery of France's Nord railway. The engine was almost certainly initially produced by Hornby's factory at Bobigny, France, and the locomotive became the prototype for the "No 3 Locomotive Series" that included the "Flying Scotsman"—see (7), *pages 42-43.* Introduced in 1927, it remained in the Hornby Catalogue until the beginning of World War II. The locomotive seen here has no smoke deflectors: this

indicates that it is an early item in the production run. The train was available in France in different liveries, including both red and black finishes, and it was sometimes sold along with standard Hornby Pullman coaches with French lettering as described below. Note that the example shown has red driving wheels, an unusual variation—but certainly not a later modification. The locomotive was made in both clockwork, as shown, and electric versions, the latter with a 4-volt (or later a 20-volt) motor: Hornby had by this time abandoned the high-voltage electric motor used in such models as the "Metropolitan Electric" (Although the "Metropolitan Electric" remained in the Catalogue for

some years thereafter). This example is in good order and is regularly run by the author (who, when a boy, particularly coveted this model but could never afford it!); however, its wheels show signs of the "metal fatigue" that is all too frequently found on Hornby items (although not invariably: it is found only in models where an incorrect mix of metals was used in casting the wheels). Length (engine and tender): 16·5in (41·91cm). The Sleeping Car (2) and Dining Car (3) are modelled on the luxury coaches provided by the International Sleeping Car Company to suit the needs of wealthy travellers to the fashionable French resorts served by the "Blue Train". Hornby's models finely reproduce the

opulence of the prototypes, with exterior finished in royal blue with gold lining and the company's famous lettering—"Compagnie Internationale des Wagons-Lits et des Grands Express Europeens" —faithfully reproduced. Both coaches have two bogies, opening end doors, working corridor connections, and celluloid windows, with printed detail of lamps on the windows of the Dining Car. Length (coach): 13in (33·02cm). The "Blue Train" is one of the most desirable items of the Hornby range and although it was in production over a long period it is now not particularly easy to find, especially in good condition, and tends to command a comparatively high price.

4-6 Gauge "0" 0-4-0 Locomotive,

numbered "1902", and Four-Wheeled Tender (6), with Twin-Bogie Passenger Coach (5), First Class, numbered "1985", and Twin-Bogie Brake Van (4); made by Gebrüder Bing, Nuremburg, Germany, and dating from around 1903. Although the coaches do not appear to be in scale with the locomotive, these items were definitely marketed together as a set. The locomotive is in spirit-fired steam (it was also available in clockwork), and its somewhat over-scale proportions were doubtless intended to give it a more powerful, longer-running performance: it is capable of running for 15-20 minutes on one filling of methylated spirit and water. Length (engine and tender): 12·75in (32·38cm). The

set shown is in London and North-Western Railway (L&NWR) livery: it was available also in the other major liveries of the period. The tinplate coaches, each with three opening doors on either side, and with interior detail of seats and compartment divisions in the Passenger Coach, are printed: in larger gauges, Bing coaches of this period were still hand-painted. Length (coach): 6·75in (17·14cm).

7-8 Gauge "0" "George the Fifth" Locomotive, numbered "2663", and Six-Wheeled Tender (8), in clockwork, by Bing: the original version, in the true-to-prototype black livery of the L&NWR and with the correct number, of the model fully described at (1) on *pages 42-43*. It is shown

here with a Brake Coach (7), numbered "1921", Third Class, of Bing's 1921 Series. These items were sold as a set, with the addition of a Passenger Coach and an oval of track. The twin-bogie coach is fitted with corridor connections and has dummy gas cylinders on its underside; it has non-opening doors and no interior detail. Length (coach): 13in (33·02cm).

9 Gauge "0" 4-4-2 Tank Locomotive, numbered "1784", by Hornby, Great Britain; this model, known as the "No 2 Special Tank", first appeared in the late 1920s and remained in production until the beginning of World War II. The example shown here is clockwork-powered, having the standard Hornby mechanism

with forward and reverse gears and brake (note the long control levers protruding from the rear of the cab), and is in the livery of the London and North Eastern Railway (LNER). The model was also available with an electric motor, and in the liveries of the other major British railway companies of the period: the London, Midland & Scottish (LMS), Great Western Railway (GWR), and Southern Railway (SR). This was a very popular Hornby item and remained in production throughout the 1930s. It is, therefore, a model that is fairly easy for the collector now to find — although it is not often to be found in the pristine condition of the example shown here. Length: 10·5in (21·94cm).

Inset (above) *This detail of the underside of the Märklin Cattle Truck shown at (1) displays the legend often stamped on these models marketed in Great Britain by Gamage's: "A. W. Gamage Ltd/Holborn/London/Made in Germany".*

1 Gauge "1" tinplate Cattle Truck, in Midland Railway livery and numbered "7804", made by Märklin, Germany, for sale in Great Britain by A. W. Gamage, dating from c1910. This item was priced at 2s 11d (14½p, 17c) in Gamage's 1911 Catalogue. Length: 8·25in (20·95cm). For the would-be collector of limited means, the rolling stock of this period offers an attractive and not too expensive field of specialisa-

tion: items like those shown here are quite often found for sale at reasonable prices.

2 Gauge "1" tinplate Cattle Truck, in Midland Railway livery and numbered "1914"; this is an item from the 1909 series made by Carette, Germany, for sale in Britain by Bassett-Lowke. It was priced in Bassett-Lowke's 1911 Catalogue at 3s 6d (17½p, 21c). Length : 8·25in (20·95cm). Note that Bassett-Lowke's price for this truck was higher than that asked by Gamage's for the very similar Märklin item shown at (1): the Märklin/Gamage series was brought out in direct rivalry with that of Carette/Bassett-Lowke. However, in the author's opinion the Märklin product, although originally lower-priced, is not

necessarily inferior to that of Carette: indeed, the Märklin items are preferred by many collectors.

3 Gauge "1" tinplate Brake Van, in Great Northern Railway livery and with the lithographed legend "Goods Break" (*sic*), made by Märklin for Gamage and bearing on the sole plate the date "1909". It was priced at 2s 11d (14½p, 17c) in the 1911 Catalogue. Length: 8·25in (20·95cm).

4 Gauge "1" tinplate Brake Van, again in Great Northern Railway livery, numbered "10959", by Carette for Bassett-Lowke, 1909 series. Compare this with (3), the Märklin interpretation of the same date. As with (1) and (2), Bassett-Lowke's price was higher: 3s 6d (17½p, 21c) in the 1911 Catalogue. Length: 8·25in

(20·95cm).

5 Gauge "1" tinplate Open Wagon in Caledonian Railway livery. This is essentially a Carette item but, like the wagon shown at (13) on *pages 44-45*, it was produced in Britain for Bassett-Lowke with the use of Carette pressings obtained after World War I. This was evidently produced in the early 1920s, since the Caledonian Railway became part of the London, Midland & Scottish Railway (LMS) in the regrouping of 1923. This wagon has a Carette number on its sole plate, but bears at one end the legend "Lithographed in England". Length: 7in (17·78cm).

6 Gauge "1" tinplate Goods Wagon in Midland Railway livery, by Märklin for Gamage, c1910. This

photograph clearly displays the distinctive Märklin couplings, a useful identification point —although it must be remembered that items of rolling stock are by no means always to be found with their original couplings. It was priced in Gamage's 1911 Catalogue at 2s 11d (14¼p, 17c). Length: 7in (17·78cm).

7 Gauge "1" tinplate Ballast Wagon, made by Bing in c1905. In spite of its English lettering, "20 Tons", this hand-painted wagon is in continental style and was not made specifically for the British market, although it was catalogued by Gamage's, at a price of 2s 0d (10p, 12c), in 1906. Available in Gauges "0", "1", "2", "3", and "4", it is a working model: small doors in the base open to

discharge ballast from the hopper body onto the track. Length: 7·75in (19·68cm).

8 Gauge "1" tinplate Hopper Wagon, lettered "City of Birmingham Gas Dept" and numbered "799", by Carette for Bassett-Lowke, 1909 series. Doors in the base open to discharge the load. This was priced at 3s 6d (17½p, 21c) in the 1911 Catalogue. Length: 7in (17·78cm).

9 Gauge "1" tinplate "Colman's Mustard Traffic" Wagon, bearing also the Norwich-based company's bull's-head trademark and the coat of arms of its Royal Warrant, by Carette for Bassett-Lowke, 1909 series. This is one of the rarer pieces from the series and is a most attractive item. It was priced at 3s 6d (17½p, 21c)

in the 1911 Catalogue. Length: 7·25in (18·4cm).

10 Gauge "1" tinplate Covered Wagon in Midland Railway livery, by Bing, c1910. A simpler model than those made by Bing for Bassett-Lowke, this was sold in Britain by Gamage's and was priced at 2s 0d (10p, 12c) in the 1911 Catalogue. It has a tarpaulin cover. Length: 7·5in (19·05cm).

11 Gauge "1" tinplate Open Wagon in Midland Railway livery, made by Märklin for Gamage, 1909, and priced at 2s 0d (10p, 12c) in the 1911 Catalogue. Length: 7in (17·78cm).

12 Gauge "1" tinplate Log Wagon, in Great Northern Railway livery and numbered "2884", made by Märklin for Gamage, 1909, and priced at 2s 11d (14½p, 17c) in

the 1911 Catalogue. Lengths of chain hold the logs in place on a tin cradle with side supports. Length: 8·5in (21·59cm).

13 Gauge "1" tinplate Bogie Timber Wagon, made by Bing in c1906 and, like (10), from the earlier series marketed in Britain by Gamage's, and priced at 2s 3d (11p, 14c) in the 1911 Catalogue. Length: 10in (25·4cm).

14 Gauge "1" tinplate Petrol Tank Wagon, lettered for the "Anglo American Oil Co Ltd" and numbered "405", made by Carette for Bassett-Lowke, 1909 series. This attractive wagon, with its securing cables of coiled wire, is a comparatively rare item in the series. It was priced at 4s 0d (20p, 24c) in the 1911 Catalogue. Length: 8·5in (21·59cm).

1 Gauge "1" Great Northern Railway 4-4-2 Atlantic Locomotive (note that the term "Atlantic" is applied to any locomotive with a 4-4-2 wheel arrangement), made by Gebrüder Bing, Nuremberg, Germany, for sale in Britain by Bassett-Lowke. This example dates from 1909, when a series of Bing models based on British prototypes and commissioned by Bassett-Lowke began to appear. These models were accurate representations of their prototypes, with very pleasing proportions. The locomotive shown was available in Gauges "0" and "1", powered by clockwork or steam. This spirit-fired steam model has twin piston-valve cylinders; Bassett-Lowke's Catalogue specifies its fittings as "covered saftey-valve, bell whistle, spring buffers, try cock, regulator in cab, vapourising spirit lamp and steam superheater", and adds that "the cylinders are lubricated by special automatic lubricator in smokebox". Length (engine and tender): 23in (58·42cm).

2 Gauge "1" Great Northern Railway 0-6-2 Tank Locomotive, numbered "190", made by Bing for Bassett-Lowke and dating from 1909. This is based on a very powerful British prototype intended for heavy suburban traffic, and Bing's careful attention to detail is apparent in the photograph. On the real locomotive, the boiler mountings had to be cut down to allow it to pass through the Metropolitan tunnels to London's Moorgate Station: this feature appears on the model. Further, since the real locomotive had to condense its own steam, again because of passing through the tunnels, a condenser pipe (the fat, black pipe at the sides) features on the model—although it is clockwork-powered and was not, in fact, available in steam. It has a two-speed, geared-wind clockwork mechanism; ie, it is wound not with a key but with a fairly sizeable crank handle—an easier, if somewhat more time-consuming, way of winding such a powerful mechanism. Although this example is in GNR livery, all Bassett-Lowke models could, for a small extra payment, be modified to suit the customer's requirements in livery and numbering. This model was available in Gauges "1" and "2", and it is interesting to note that a fair number of Gauge "2" examples in fine condition have appeared for sale in recent years. Length: 13·75in (34·92cm).

3 Gauge "1" 0-4-0 Tank Engine, by Bing for Bassett-Lowke. This is the Gauge "1" version, 10in (25·4cm) long, of the celebrated "No 112" tank locomotive available in Gauges "0", "1", and "2", in steam, clockwork, and electric, from c1910 until 1930. Like all steam models, which obviously must withstand hard wear, this example is hand-painted. It was originally available in the liveries of the Midland; London and North-Western (L&NWR); Great Northern (GNR); and

Caledonian (blue) Railways, and later in the colours of the London, Midland & Scottish (LMS); London and North Eastern (LNER); Great Western (GWR); and Southern (SR) Railways. This example has obviously been well-steamed, but it is still apparent that it is in SR livery, dating it to the mid-1920s after the regrouping of the British railway companies. Note the large control levers at the rear of the cab: a thoughtful provision to save the owner from burned hands. Another interesting point is that the number "112" is the number of Bassett-Lowke's store in High Holborn, London.

4 Gauge "1" Lancashire & Yorkshire Railway 4-6-0 Locomotive, numbered "1510", and Six-Wheeled Tender, made by Bing for Bassett-Lowke. A most pleasing representation of an Aspinall-designed prototype, this is a very rare item: it was first catalogued in 1915, very soon after the appearance of the prototype, and it is believed that only 100 were made. Of the six examples encountered by the author, all were in excellent condition, showing that this was a model that was treasured right from the start. It was available in clockwork only, with a powerful two-speed, six-coupled (ie, driving all six of the larger wheels) geared-wind mechanism. As on the prototype the driving wheels are comparatively small, giving excellent hauling power. Overall length of engine and tender:

22in (55·88cm).

5 Gauge "1" 0-4-0 Peckett Saddle Tank Locomotive, numbered "101". This is the early and very desirable version made by Carette, Nuremberg, and dating from 1906, of a powerful shunting engine built by Peckett of Bristol. Carette ceased production in 1917, and Bing later made a version for Bassett-Lowke using parts acquired from Carette. It was made by Carette in Gauges "0", "1", and "2"; by Bing probably only in Gauges "0" and "1". This example, 11in (27·94cm) long, is in Midland Railway livery and has a particularly long-running clockwork mechanism. The Carette version is rare; the Bing version is more common.

6 Gauge "1" 4-4-2 Atlantic Tank Locomotive in London, Brighton & South Coast Railway livery, numbered "11", by Bing for Bassett-Lowke. Available also in Gauge "0", this model had a long run, appearing in c1912 and remaining in Bassett-Lowke's Catalogue (with a break, of course, during World War I) until the late 1920s, when it was available in SR livery. It has a powerful two-speed, four-coupled clockwork mechanism and is well-detailed. Märklin produced a similar model, in Gauges "0" and "1", which is a less accurate representation and has a more "toy-like" quality, making it generally more desirable to collectors. This Bing version, which is 15·75in (40cm) long, is not particularly rare.

1 Gauge "1" Gotthard 0-4-4-0 BO-BO Locomotive of Swiss Railways, numbered "1802", made by Gebrüder Märklin, Germany, immediately after World War I. ("BO-BO" refers to the wheel arrangement and signifies that the locomotive has two bogies, each with four wheels). This model was first catalogued by Märklin in 1919 and was available also in Gauge "0"; production continued throughout the 1920s, but it was probably not made in any great quantity: production is more likely to be numbered in the hundreds rather than thousands. A massive and imposing model for three-rail electric operation, it is hand-painted and nicely detailed, with working headlights, opening doors at the ends, and dummy pantographs on the roof. The roof lifts off to give access to the powerful 110-220 volt electric motor. This model was made primarily for the continental market, but it is now much in demand by collectors all over the world and is particularly popular with American collectors: an attractive, desirable, and rare item. Length: 17·7in (45cm).

2-4 Gauge "1" Steeple-Cab 0-4-0 Locomotive (2), numbered "V 1021"; with (3) Four-Wheeled Suburban Coach ("Personenwagen"), numbered "18071", shown also at (5) on *pages 52-53,* where a detailed description is given; and (4), Four-Wheeled Passenger Luggage Van, numbered "18081". This train in continental livery was made by Märklin around 1930. The Steeple-Cab is based on a locomotive of the Paris-Orleans Railway: the prototype was, of course, electric, but the model is clockwork, with a very powerful Märklin two-speed mechanism: note the brake and forward/reverse controls protruding from the cab, and the speed regulator on the roof. The locomotive's detail includes cast-metal headlights and chrome-plated handrails. The Passenger Luggage Van (4) has sliding doors centrally and opening doors towards its end, and is fitted with red rearlights that can be illuminated. The raised part of its roof accommodates a guard's lookout. Lengths (locomotive): 10in (25·4cm); (rolling stock): 10·5in (26·67cm).

5 Gauge "1" tinplate Four-Wheeled Crane Truck by Gebrüder Bing, Nuremburg, Germany; the odd one out on this spread, where all other items are by Bing's great rival Märklin. This model was sold in Great Britain by A.W. Gamage, London: in Gamage's 1906 Catalogue it was listed in Gauges "0", "1", "2", and "3"; the Gauge "1" version being priced at 2s 3d (11p, 13c). As usual for its period, it is hand-painted. As is apparent, the crane is fully pivoted on the truck body; mounted just behind the bottom of the jib is a counterbalance weight that moves forward or back on a slide. The hook (missing from this example) is raised and lowered manually

by a crank handle. Lengths (truck body): 5·5in (13·97cm); (overall, including jib arm): 8·75in (22·2cm).

6 Gauge "1" tinplate Cattle Truck by Märklin, catalogued by Gamage's in 1906 in Gauges "0", "1", and "2", and priced then at 5s 6d (27½p, 33c) in Gauge "1". Hand-painted, it has sliding doors centrally on either side and a hinged roof; the ubiquitous Märklin bogies of the period are seen to advantage in the photograph. The legend "Made in Germany" is stamped on the base. The example shown is of particular interest to American collectors, since it was intended for the US market, with the letters "P.R.R." ("Pennsylvania Railroad") stamped at each end. Length: 9·5in

(24·13cm).

7 Gauge "1" North British Railway Atlantic (4-4-2) Locomotive, numbered "4021" and Six-Wheeled Tender, first catalogued by Märklin in 1919. This example was obviously intended for the British market, but Märklin also produced it for the continental market in German (*Deutschbahn*) livery of black with red wheels. However, why Märklin should have chosen a prototype from a comparatively obscure British railway of the period remains something of a mystery. This model was available in steam, as shown here, clock-work, and electric versions, in Gauges "0" and "1". It has the unfortunate Märklin characteristic of being extremely heavy and, in consequence, is not a good

runner, seeming only just able to drag itself around the track! Nevertheless, it is an impressive and quite handsome locomotive, with such detail as brass handrails and simulated coal in the tender. Note the oiling caps situated on top of the cylinders, a typical Märklin feature. Length (engine and tender): 23in (58·42cm).

8 Gauge "1" 0-6-0 Tank Locomotive; a somewhat rare version, as explained below, of a popular model first made by Märklin after 1918 and produced in Gauges "0" and "1" over a long period. This example is in clockwork: note the large control levers (only one visible here) protruding from the sides of the cab, and the rim brakes (just visible) acting on the front pair of wheels. It is

12in (30·48cm) long. First appearing immediately after World War I, it was probably available in the liveries of all the major British railway companies — certainly in those of the Great Western Railway (GWR) and London and North Eastern Railway (LNER) — but the author has not been able to locate any instance of the example shown here, in Great Eastern Railway (GER) livery, having been catalogued. The model was sold in Great Britain by both Gamage's and by Bond's ("Bond's o' Euston Road"), London: up to World War I, Gamage's appear to have had a near-exclusive arrangement for marketing Märklin's products in London, but after the War Bond's were also selling Märklin's models.

1-4 Gauge "0" "American Flyer Lines" 2-4-2 Locomotive and Bogie Tender (4), with Gondola (3), Breakdown Crane (2), and Caboose (1). This train by the American Flyer company, USA, is in near-mint condition and dates from about 1929. The locomotive, for three-rail electric operation, has a diecast body with a brass handrail and domes and piping in copper-coloured tinplate. It is fitted with forward and reverse mechanism and has a working headlight. The tender, with two bogies, is tinplate, with copper-coloured detail and a top that simulates coal. The tinplate, two-bogie Gondola has a dummy brakewheel at its forward end. The Breakdown Crane, again tinplate with two bogies, has a jib

that can be raised and lowered and is held in the desired position by a latch that engages with holes pierced in the cab roof. The tinplate, two-bogie Caboose features a conductor's lookout; when the train is running, the rear bogie picks up current from the track to illuminate the interior of the caboose. Like the locomotive and tender, the brightly painted (ie, dipped) rolling stock is liberally adorned with "American Flyer Lines" transfers. American collectors, to whom this item will be of most interest, will probably be able to find models of this kind without great difficulty, but they are not widely collected outside the USA. Lengths (engine and tender): 15·5in (39·37cm); (rolling stock,

each): 10in (25·4cm).

5-6 Gauge "0" Coaches by Gebrüder Bing, Nuremburg, Germany; described as "Pullmans", these appeared in Bing's English-language Catalogue of 1926. The pair comprises a Pullman Dining Coach (5), numbered "3295", and a Composite Passenger and Guards Van (6), numbered "3296". They were available in the liveries of the Great Western Railway (GWR), as shown, London, Midland & Scottish Railway (LMS), and London and North Eastern Railway (LNER). It is of interest to compare these with the earlier Bing coaches shown on *pages 50-51*. At this comparatively late date, the coaches still have detailed interiors with tables and chairs

(with spikes for passengers, although passenger figures had not been available for some years), and opening doors. Length: 12in (30·48cm).

7 Gauge "0" "Duke of York" 4-4-0 Locomotive and Six-Wheeled Tender, numbered "1931", made by Bing for Bassett-Lowke, Great Britain. Made both in clockwork, as shown (note key on tender), and electric, this model was first issued in 1927 and was produced under an arrangement with B.D.V. Cigarettes: the locomotive and tender, wagons, coaches, rails, and accessories, could be obtained by collecting coupons given to the purchasers of the cigarettes—the locomotive "cost" 260 coupons, the tender 150 coupons. Locomotive and tender

could be purchased in the normal way at an inclusive price of £1 5s 0d (£1.25, $1.50), or £1 16s 0d (£1.80, $2.16) for a locomotive fitted with Bassett-Lowke's "Permag" electric motor. The number "1931" may be taken as the date of production: the model is also found with the numbers "1927", "1928", "1929", and "1930". Shown in LMS livery, it was also available in the colours of the GWR, LNER, and Southern Railway (SR). This model was made by Winteringham, Bassett-Lowke's Northampton-based subsidiary. Length (engine and tender): 14·75in (37·46cm).

8-10 Gauge "0" 0-4-0 Locomotive and Four-Wheeled Tender, both numbered "504", with two Four-Wheeled Passenger Coaches

(9-10), First Class, both numbered "3747"; from a fairly late series made by Bing for the British market, 1926. These were sold in the UK as a boxed set, with an oval of track, at a price of £1 3s 0d (£1.15, $1.38), and were available in the major railway liveries; the example shown is in LNER colours. The clockwork-powered locomotive has forward/reverse mechanism. Note the unusual couplings on the coaches, a feature that appeared on a number of items around this time. The same coaches, but finished in the livery of a Germany railway, appeared in Bing's German catalogue. Lengths (engine and tender): 11·5in (29·21cm); (coach): 4·75in (12·06cm).

11 Gauge "0" "Vulcan" 0-4-0

clockwork Locomotive, numbered "3433" and Four-Wheeled Tender, by Bing; much like (8) and dating from the same period, but of slightly heavier construction with a pleasing brass dome and sturdy polished handrails. Like (7), this was available by an arrangement with B.D.V. Cigarettes and could be obtained by collecting coupons. The example shown is in GWR livery. Length (engine and tender): 11·5in (29·21cm).

12-14 Gauge "0" "King Edward VII" 0-4-0 clockwork Locomotive, numbered "1902", and Four-Wheeled Tender (14), with Four-Wheeled Passenger Coach (13), and Brake Van (12); again by Bing, but considerably earlier than (8-10) or (11), and

probably dating from about 1906. It is in London and North-Western Railway (L&NWR) livery. Lengths (engine and tender): 10·75in (27·3cm); (coaches): 5in (12·7cm).

15-16 Gauge "0" "Minerva" 0-4-0 (no connecting rods) clockwork Locomotive, numbered "3410", and Four-Wheeled Tender (16), with a Four-Wheeled Passenger Coach (15), First/Third Class; another simple model produced by Bing in the mid-1920s. These are in LNER livery. Lengths (engine and tender): 9in (22·86cm); (coach): 4·75in (12·06cm). Compare the locomotive with the simple 0-4-0 clockwork engine of Bing's earlier period, dating from about 1906, in L&NWR livery, shown just behind and to the rear of the coach at (16).

1

3

5

4

1 Gauge "1" tinplate Twelve-Wheeled LMS Dining Car, numbered "13210". In its original form, this coach was made in the 1909 series produced by Carette, Nuremburg, Germany, for sale in Great Britain by Bassett-Lowke. It is based on an early 20th-century Dining Car that was used on the west coast routes of the London and North-Western Railway (L&NWR), and appeared in L&NWR livery in Bassett-Lowke's pre-World War I catalogues. However, the fact that this example is lithographed in the livery of the London, Midland & Scotland Railway (LMS) shows that it dates from the mid-1920s, following the regrouping of the British railway companies that made the L&NWR part of the LMS, and that it was,

therefore, made for Bassett-Lowke at Northampton from Carette pressings acquired after World War I; Carette, French-owned but German-based, having ceased production in 1917. It was, in fact, made by George Winteringham, who had designed for Bassett-Lowke the celebrated "Lowke" track. This designer established the business known as Winteringham Ltd at Northampton as early as 1900: the firm's total output went to Bassett-Lowke. Available also in Gauge "0", it features opening doors at both ends, provision for corridor connections, and dummy gas cylinders fitted beneath the body. The roof slides off, but there are no interior fittings. Length: 19·5in (49·53cm).

2 Gauge "1" tinplate Bogie Passenger Coach, First/Third Class, in Great Western Railway livery and numbered "132-24"—which is, in fact, not the number of the coach, but a catalogue number—made by Carette for Bassett-"Lowko" track. This designer 12·5in (31·75cm) long and of the type designated by the author a "bogie shorty", was available, like the rest of the series, in both Gauges "0" and "1" and in the liveries of the five major British railway companies of the period: Great Western (GWR), as seen here; Midland (MR); Great Northern (GNR); London and North-Western (L&NWR); and London and South-Western (L&SWR). It is nicely lithographed and has four opening doors

on each side, with a single dummy gas cylinder fitted on the underside. The roof slides off, but there are no interior fittings. It was priced at 6s 0d (30p, 36c) in Bassett-Lowke's 1911 Catalogue.

3 Gauge "1" tinplate Six-Wheeled Passenger Coach, First/Third Class, in Midland Railway livery and numbered "13213", again a catalogue number rather than the number of a coach, made by Carette for Bassett-Lowke in c1911. The wheel arrangement of this coach mirrors a real practice of the time in that it incorporates the Clemenson design: the six wheels are mounted on radial trucks and can thus easily follow the sharpest curves on the track. It has nicely-lithographed roof detail; the roof is removable,

but no interior fittings other than a tinplate division between the First and Third Class compartments are provided. Available in Gauges "0", "1", and "2", this coach was advertised in the Bassett-Lowke catalogue issued just before World War I, at a price of 6s 6d (32½p, 39c) for the Gauge "2" model. Length: 10·5in (26·67cm).

4 Gauge "1" tinplate Full Brake Van, in London and South-Western Railway livery and numbered "No. 133", made by Carette for Bassett-Lowke, 1909 series. It was available also in the liveries of the other four major British railway companies of the time—see caption (2)—but in the author's opinion this is the most attractive livery of the series. It is also the rarest and the

hardest for the collector to find today. This coach has non-opening doors and no interior fittings; dummy gas cylinders are fitted to the underside. Available also in Gauge "0", this item was first catalogued by Bassett-Lowke in 1909, at a price of 8s 0d (40p, 48c) for the Gauge "1" version. For a nominal charge, Bassett-Lowke would supply the coaches of this series with scale couplings; however, for fitting turned cast-iron wheels, which would certainly give much better running quality, an added charge of 3s 6d (17½p, 21c)—an increase of nearly 50 per cent on the catalogue price—was demanded. For a further extra charge, Bassett-Lowke would paint any item in any livery that the customer might require: he could

make up his own livery if he so desired! Thus, it is possible that from time to time the collector may encounter items in quite unusual colour schemes. Length: 16in (40·64cm).

5 Gauge "1" tinplate Bogie Passenger Coach, Third Class, in Great Northern Railway livery and numbered "1321", made by Carette for Bassett-Lowke, 1909 series. In all except lithography and layout, this coach resembles (4); catalogue and price details are also the same. Again, it was available in the five major British railway liveries and in Gauges "0" and "1". All the coaches of Carette's 1909 series were produced in pairs: as a Full Brake and as a Passenger Coach. They were also made in shorter

bogie versions, as six-wheelers, and as twelve-wheelers. Length: 16in (40·64cm).

6 Gauge "1" tinplate Brake Van, in London and North-Western Railway livery and numbered "13912", made by Carette for Bassett-Lowke, 1909 series. This is the Brake Van version of the Passenger Coach shown at (3), and again has its six wheels fitted in accordance with the Clemenson design. It has non-opening doors and is not provided with any interior fittings. Although it is not immediately apparent in the photograph, the end windows stand away from the body of the van to provide a guard's look-out post. Length: 10·5in (26·67cm).

Inset (above) *The rear of the tender of the locomotive shown at (3) bears a transfer with the Bassett-Lowke "LOWKO" trademark. This trademark was used before 1914 and, from time to time, in the 1920s; however, not all items marketed in Great Britain by Bassett-Lowke bear the firm's mark.*

1 Gauge "1" 4-4-4 Bavarian State Railway Locomotive and Eight-Wheeled Tender, made by Gebrüder Bing, Nuremberg, Germany, from 1912 until World War I and again, although only in limited numbers, in the early 1920s, in Gauge "1" only and probably from parts made before the War. This large—overall length with tender: 27·5in

(69·85cm)—and powerful locomotive is an externally-spirit-fired steam model with a vaporising burner; ie, the spirit is vaporised before it is ignited, which is, in theory at any rate, a more efficient system. Built for the continental market and available in Gauges "0" and "1", steam only, it was not generally sold in Great Britain. However, although production of this model was not resumed by Bing after World War I, it made a brief appearance in the Bassett-Lowke Catalogue for 1924: the "bargain price" of £6 6s 0d (£6·30, $7·56), reduced from £8 8s 0d (£8·40, $10·08), suggests that there was little demand in Britain, where it remains a rare item in Gauge "1", and

extremely rare in Gauge "0", for a German-style locomotive.
2 Gauge "1" 4-6-0 Locomotive, named "Sir Sam Fay" and numbered "423", and Six-Wheeled Tender, made by Bing for sale in Great Britain by Bassett-Lowke. Catalogued immediately prior to the outbreak of World War I in 1914, at about the same time as the appearance of its prototype (a Great Central Railway locomotive bearing the name of a director of that railway), it did not appear in any quantity until the 1920s. Unusually for items made by Bing for Bassett-Lowke, this example bears beneath the tender a Bing trademark, with the words "Made in Bavaria". It was available in both clockwork and electric versions, in Gauge "1"

only: the example shown has a powerful six-coupled, geared-wind clockwork mechanism, with the usual control levers protruding from the rear of the cab. As with several other models made by Bing for Bassett-Lowke at this period, no tinplate coaches were produced to go with the locomotive—although customers could have matching rolling stock painted to order by Bassett-Lowke, usually from the standard Bing/Bassett-Lowke coaches of the time and most likely in GWR form, of which Bassett-Lowke then appears to have had a surfeit. The attractively-finished model proved popular: it is believed that up to 1,000 examples were made, and it is thus an item that the collector may well

encounter. When the example shown came into the author's possession it was in a poor state: as seen now, it is the result of careful professional restoration, which included the repainting of the entire boiler, the side frames, and nameplates. Overall length of engine and tender: 24·25in (61·6cm).

3 Gauge "1" 0-6-0 Locomotive and Six-Wheeled Tender, numbered "3044", made by Bing for Bassett-Lowke. First catalogued in 1911, and available in Gauge "0" and "1", clockwork-powered versions only, it was then priced at £3 3s 0d (£3·15, $3·78). It did not reappear after World War I, and is thus a fairly rare item. Based on the L&NWR so-called "Cauliflower" locomotive,

and available, as shown, authentically in L&NWR livery, it has a two-speed mechanism with forward-reverse gears and brake. On the example shown the original mechanism has been modified with a Van Reimsdijk speed-control system, enabling the locomotive to be run at a very slow speed and thus giving a most realistic effect with a long line of wagons. Overall length of engine and tender: 18·5in (47cm).

4 Gauge "1" 4-4-0 Great Western Railway (GWR) Locomotive, named "County of Northampton", and Six-Wheeled Tender, made by Bing for Bassett-Lowke and dating from 1909. It was made as a steam model only, in Gauges "1" and "2" (with a very small number made in Gauge

"3"). Total production is believed to have been around 500 models, the majority in Gauge "1", and although fairly rare it may be found at auction from time to time. It may be noted that the GWR had, in reality, no locomotive named "County of Northampton", for the lines of that railway ran nowhere near the East Midlands' county; however, Bassett-Lowke's factory was situated in Northampton and the firm doubtless desired to honour the locality in this manner! The example shown here is of particular interest in that it formed part of the estate of the late Victor Harrison, a member of a famous printing family and a personal friend of Wenman J. Bassett-Lowke. This

loco, among the first of the series, was sent by Bing to Bassett-Lowke for evaluation and was presented by W. J. Bassett-Lowke to his old friend. It has been regularly run throughout its long life: since coming into the author's possession some twenty years ago, it has steamed many thousand Gauge "1" miles and is still in splendid working order. The overall length of engine and tender is 21in (53·34cm).

5 Gauge "1" Coal Wagon by Bing, made for the German market in c1906. This four-wheeled tinplate wagon in attractive orange livery has a pressed-tin top painted to simulate a full load of coal; stamped on the side is the legend "10000Kg", indicating its capacity. It is 8in (20·32cm) long.

1 Gauge "1" 4-6-2 PLM (Paris, Lyon and Mediterranée Railway) Pacific Locomotive (any locomotive with a 4-6-2 wheel arangement is designated a Pacific) and Eight-Wheeled Tender, (twin bogies), made by Märklin, Germany. This model first appeared in 1912 and was available in various forms—in Gauges "0" and "1", and in steam (as shown), clockwork, and electric versions—until 1930. It was generally marketed only on the continent—although it could be ordered in Great Britain through A. W. Gamage, London—and it appeared both in dark green livery, as shown, and in black. The locomotive is of typical continental appearance and is well-detailed. However,

Märklin have been inclined to spoil the realism of an otherwise pleasing model by incongruously siting the filler and safety valves on top of the domes instead of directly on the boiler as in the prototype. Note the automatic lubricators for the cylinders above the front bogies. The miniature spring-loaded hand pump on the side of the locomotive is used to pump water from a track-side tank to the boiler, via a length of rubber tubing: in practice, it does not work very well. Note also the screw-cap on the tender: spirit is poured in here and fed through rubber tubing from the inlet pipe (see *Inset*) in the cab; the wheel at the front of the tender controls the admission of the

spirit. Although most attractive and impressive in their steam versions, these large Märklin locomotives do not run very satisfactorily because of their excessive weight, the frames being of cast metal. Nevertheless, they are much desired by collectors and are rare in Britain. Overall length of engine and tender is 28·75in (73cm).
2 Gauge "1" 4-6-2 Maffei Pacific Locomotive and Eight-Wheeled Tender (twin bogies), by Gebrüder Bing, Nuremburg, dating from 1912. It is a splendid model, based on a prototype by the German builder Maffei and finished in the black-and-red livery of the Bavarian State Railway —and this particular example is of especial interest. The pointed

top of the cab is typical of the type and, in a continental-style locomotive, one would expect the boiler front also to be pointed —as in the Gebrüder Bing 4-4-0 Bavarian State Railway locomotive shown at (1) on *pages 66-67*—instead of rounded, as seen here. The author has never seen the model catalogued in the form shown here and, indeed, has encountered no other expert who has. It is the author's opinion that this particular example was intended for the North American market, where it would have appeared without buffers and with the addition of a cowcatcher. However, the tender, which is almost certainly the one originally supplied, is of

typically German appearance. This model must, therefore, be described as an interesting hybrid, the exact nature of which remains something of a mystery. In its usual form, with a pointed boiler, it had a long production run in Gauges "0" and "1": it was made in steam, electric, and clockwork versions, and the Gauge "1" version in steam was still being catalogued by Bing in 1927. The six-coupled mechanism of the example shown is driven by a simple electric motor of the early type, and it features electric headlights. Note that the central pair of driving wheels is unflanged to enable it to negotiate sharp curves: this is a common feature on larger Bing locomotives of the period

but it does not appear in equivalent models by Märklin. Bassett-Lowke always insisted that locomotives made in Germany for the British market should have unflanged central wheels, and when Bing, in 1910, produced a Mogul (ie, with 2-6-0 wheel arrangement) with flanged central wheels it was rejected by Bassett-Lowke and was marketed instead by Gamage's. Length of engine and tender: 27in (68·58cm).

3 Gauge "1" 4-6-2 Locomotive and Eight-Wheeled Tender by Märklin, made for the British market and dating from the late 1920s. This is Märklin's massive and somewhat freelance representation of the famous "Flying Scotsman" of the London and

North Eastern Railway (LNER): it is an example of Märklin's usual cavalier attitude to both the prototype and to numbering. Although some attempt has been made with the tapered boiler to give a characteristic LNER appearance, neither the cab nor the twin-bogie tender bear any resemblance to the prototype. The number "1021" is the Märklin code referring to the gauge (shown by the final digit): the number of the prototype was "4472". It is, nevertheless, a most impressive model, with an overall length (engine and tender) of 29in (73·66cm). It was made in Gauges "0" and "1", in steam only: its mechanism is much like that of the PLM Pacific shown at (1), incorporating

Märklin's unique firing system with its vaporising spirit lamp. First catalogued by Gamage's in 1928, it remained available only until the early 1930s, and because of this short production run is now very rare. It is a much-desired item.

Inset (top right) *A closeup view of the cab of the Märklin PLM Pacific locomotive shown at (1) shows the steam pressure gauge (bearing the initials "GM&Co.", and with a water gauge hidden behind it); speed regulator; inlet pipe for spirit (see main caption); and try cock. The last-named—the curved pipe descending to the right in the photograph—is used to test the pressure of the steam.*

1 Gauge "0" 4-4-0 Midland Railway Locomotive and Six-Wheeled Tender, numbered "1000", made by Gebrüder Bing, Nuremberg, Germany, for sale in Great Britain by Bassett-Lowke. This little locomotive had a short production run just before World War I. It is one of Bing's better-proportioned British-outline Gauge "0" steam models—and had it been given the correct Belpaire firebox it would be a fairly accurate model of one of the famous Midland Railway Compounds. As in most Bing steam locomotives using the pot-boiler firing method (in which a methylated-spirit-fired lamp actually burns visibly on the underside of the boiler barrel), the central boiler is liable to

scorching, flaking and discolouring. Like some other Gauge "0" and certain Gauge "1" models, this has its spirit reservoir in the tender: a flexible connection controlled by a needle-valve supplies the vaporising burner head. Length (engine and tender): 15·75in (40·005cm).

2 Gauge "0" 4-4-2 Precursor-Type Tank Locomotive, numbered "6810", in London, Midland & Scottish Railway (LMS) livery; originally produced by Bing—see (4)—this is an electric model produced by Bassett-Lowke in c1925. These locomotives had a long production run and were made in great numbers. The example shown is one of the first run of British-made locomotives and is one of Bassett-Lowke's overpaints of

the earlier and more attractive London and North-Western Railway (L&NWR) livery—see (4). Most of the LMS Precursors were, in fact, issued in LMS "passenger red": it is possible that this example was painted to order, or it may represent a Bassett-Lowke experiment. Close examination will reveal the overpainted boiler-lining, as compared with (4). This example started life as a clockwork model—the farther side of the locomotive displays a professionally-blocked keyhole —but although an interesting and unusual feature, this conversion gives it no significant added value. Length: 11·625in (29·53cm).

3 Gauge "0" 4-2-2 Midland Railway Locomotive and Six-Wheeled Tender, numbered "650";

a 4-volt electric model made by Bing and marketed in Great Britain by Gamage's and, probably, for a short time by Bassett-Lowke. The model appeared before World War I in clockwork and electric, the latter being much rarer, and production may have resumed briefly post-War (although there may have been a re-issue of pre-War stock). This little locomotive, quite nicely representing one of the Midland Railway's Johnson Single-Wheelers, is one of Bing's most charming early lithographed items. It is quite rare and may be considered as a classic of its kind: it is eagerly sought and most collectors would wish to have one. Length (engine and tender): 15·75in (40·005cm).

4 Gauge "0" 4-4-2 Precursor-Type Tank Locomotive, numbered "44", in L&NWR livery, made by Bing for Bassett-Lowke; see (2) for more details. These are among the easier Bing/Bassett-Lowke locomotives to find, but are desirable when in good condition. Märklin's similar tank engines of the same period, again in Gauges "0" and "1", are a little harder to find, although still not rare. Length: 11·5in (29·21cm).

5 Gauge "0" Eight-Wheeled Restaurant Car, Great Western Railway (GWR), by Exley, Great Britain, dating from c1949. Exley is best known for its series of coaches produced from the mid-1930s onward, which usually have aluminium body

wrappers, cast ends, wooden floors, real glass windows, and card interiors, (seats, dividers, etc). These pre-War vehicles were entirely hand-finished—even the letters and numbers were hand-applied—with the result that some look quite smart and others extremely crude! The example seen here, however, is one of the post-War run. in GWR livery. It is perhaps unfortunate that after World War II Exley to a large extend standardized the body types of its vehicles, basing them on main-line LMS Stanier stock: the vehicles are thus acceptable in LMS colours but may look a little odd in others. Generally, however, they show a great improvement in quality and finish over their pre-War

counterparts. Exley would build almost any passenger vehicle to order and also produced small numbers of locomotives and wagons. The firm's vehicles seem to rank rather low on the collecting scale, although they sometimes attract higher prices simply because they can be used to make up superb trains with many Bassett-Lowke locomotives. Length: 16·5in (41·91cm).

6 Gauge "0" 4-6-0 "Pendennis Castle" Locomotive, numbered "4079", and Six-Wheeled Tender, in GWR livery; a 12-volt electric model by Bassett-Lowke (V. Reader). After World War II, Bassett-Lowke engaged Mr V. Hunt to build its more detailed and expensive models in brass. The range included GWR "Castles",

"Kings", and Prairie Tanks; British Railways (BR) "Britannias"; an LMS 2-8-0; and some others. These hand-built models varied in quality but, although not superbly painted, were generally attractive. Some purchasers were dissatisfied, however, and subsequently Mr V. Reader rebuilt and improved certain Hunt models (and some pre-War non-Hunt types). The Hunt-designed, Reader-rebuilt locomotive shown here testifies to Reader's great skill: it is a beautifully-proportioned model —the paintwork being the work of the present owner. It is an extremely desirable item, both as a collectable model in its own right and as an example of model engineering. Length (engine and tender): 18in (45·72cm).

1 Gauge "0" Two-Car Diesel Unit, "Flying Hamburger", Serial Number TW12970; a 20-volt AC electric model by Gebrüder Märklin, Göppingen, Germany, produced from the early 1930s until World War II. During the 1930s, German railways introduced many high-speed, multi-unit diesel trains, and this painted tinplate model is one of a series made at that time by Märklin. It was available in Gauges "0" and "1", in clockwork or electric. Like some of their American-made counterparts by Lionel, these articulated sets had special motorized units: in this example, the motorized unit is situated at the mid-point where the two end vehicles are hinged. The model features operating head- and tail-lamps. Although not to the taste of all collectors, these stream-lined sets are very eagerly sought after, and they are not too hard to find in comparison with some other Märklin items. Length: 19·685in (50cm).

2 Gauge "0" "Talbot" Hopper Wagon (*Schotterwagen*), Serial No 1767, made in c1938. Beautifully made of soldered tinplate, this is a delightful model, with pivoted doors that open to discharge the load, and such detail as strengthening channels, end rails, ladder, and rivets. A Gauge "1" version was also produced in the early 1930s. Märklin wagons in this series are avidly collected and are so valued for their realism by model railway enthusiasts that in recent years some, including the one shown, have been made in replica by Hehr of Stuttgart, Germany. Length: 6·5in (16·5cm).

3 Gauge "0" Bogie Tank Wagon (*Kesselwagen*), "Shell", Serial No 1854S, dating from c1937. Märklin produced a fine range of these bogie tank vehicles throughout the 1930s. They had excellent play value: the top fillers unscrew so that the tank can be filled, and it can be emptied through the somewhat over-scale tap at the side. However, steel or tinplate-bodied vehicles that have been filled with water are subsequently liable to corrosion, and many of these highly collectable wagons will now be found with badly-rusted lower bodies. Length: 9·65in (24·5cm).

4 Gauge "0" Banana Wagon (*Bananenwagen*), "Fyffes", Serial No 1792, dating from the 1930s. This is one of Märklin's attractive lithographed and embossed wagons. Like most Märklin vehicles it is highly collectable, and it is not among the hardest to find. A Gauge "1" version was also made. Length: 7·28in (18·5cm).

5 Gauge "0" *Seefische* (Fish) Wagon: one of a Märklin series of the mid-1920s, made in Gauge "0" and "1". The vehicle is soldered, with stencilled artwork and rubber-stamped lettering: Märklin retained these methods for much longer than its great rival, Bing, which adopted lithography at a much earlier date. This charming vehicle has sliding central doors —but the hinged door fitted to the raised cabin suggests a

railway worker of pygmy size! Some wagons of this desirable series are very hard to find. Length: 6·375in (16·19cm).

6 Gauge "0" Four-Wheeled Electric Locomotive, Serial No RS66/12910; a 20-volt electric model, and one of the smallest of a fine range of Swiss-type, electric-outline locomotives (produced in both electric and clockwork versions) made by Märklin from the early 1930s until World War II. The example shown, with working headlights and rather austere pressed-tinplate pantographs, was one of the last in the range: although decidedly short, it thoroughly captures the style of the prototype. The electric version, as shown, utilizes a complex sequence-reversing system in conjunction

with the field of the motor—Hornby and Lionel pursued similar systems —and gives an excellent performance. Length: 8·46in (21·5cm).

7 Gauge "0" "Mitropa" Dining Car (*Speisewagen*), Serial No 1942G, dating from 1939; one of a superb series of mainline corridor coaches made by Märklin in several European liveries, including German national green, French "Wagons-Lits" blue, and the German "Mitropa" version as shown. The coaches were obtainable with or without interior detail, from the early 1930s until World War II. They are true classics of their kind, with high-quality lithography and featuring such detail as opening doors, roof access ladders and platforms, correct vents, side rails, battery

boxes, and more. Flexible corridor connections were provided, and hinged roofs give access to the interior. This series is so eagerly sought in Europe and the USA that Hehr of Germany and Darstead of Switzerland have recently produced replicas. Length: 15·75in (40cm).

8 Gauge "0" 4-6-2 01-Type Pacific Locomotive and Eight-Wheeled (two bogies) Tender; a model with 20-volt AC reversing electric motor, available from Märklin from the mid-1930s until World War II. A magnificent model of a German express passenger locomotive, with working headlamps and through connection for coach lighting, this is one of a classic series that included the 4-8-2 ME "Mountain Class", the Borsig

Streamliner, and the US-outline "Commodore Vanderbilt" and "New York Central Hudson". These are perhaps the most collectable of all model locomotives of the 1930s and are avidly sought after. The model shown is probably the least rare of the series, but will still be costly and hard to find. Length (engine and tender): 20·67in (52·5cm).

9 Station Newspaper Trolley, Serial No 2628: one of Märklin's delightful accessories available throughout the 1930s. Too large for Gauge "0" use, or even Gauge "1", this is a truly fine toy. This example is complete with all eight of its original miniature printed newspaper fronts, and in this condition is very rare. Length: 4·33in (11cm); width; 1·77in (4·5cm).

1 Gauge "0" Eight-Wheeled Bogie Passenger Coach, in SCNF (French National Railways) colours, issued by Hornby, Bobigny-Seine, France, after World War II to complement the streamlined, steam-outline 4-4-2 locomotive of the period. This vehicle, with its distinctive windows, appears a little low in proportion but is a fairly accurate model of a contemporary French coach. It is strange that whereas the Gauge "0" production of Hornby, Great Britain, was severely limited after World War II, French Hornby's Gauge "0" programme continued to thrive for some years. Like most French Hornby items, these coaches are quite eagerly sought after and are not very easy to find. Length: 12in (30·48cm).

2 Gauge "0" Wagons-Lits Pullman Dining Car, by Jep, France, made throughout the 1930s and again, briefly, after World War II. The famous French "Flèche d'Or" (Golden Arrow) express ran a unique set of Wagons-Lits Pullmans, and the "golden arrows" are evident on the waist of this model, one of Jep's finest items. Although a little over-scale and somewhat short, this fully captures the spirit of its prototype, with the aid of fine lithographed detail and good door-end design. Like their companion "Nord" locomotives, these coaches are extremely collectable and quite hard for the collector to find. Length: 14in (35·56cm).

3 Gauge "0" "Nord" Bogie Baggage Container Vehicle, "Flèche d'Or",

by Jep; like (2), this was available throughout the 1930s and again, briefly, post-War. This vehicle, delightfully modelled by Jep, was unique to the "Flèche d'Or" express: it had detachable end baggage containers which were shipped across the Channel to run on the British "Golden Arrow" from Dover to Victoria, London. Quite rare, this model is equally as collectable as (2); indeed, they may almost be seen as a matching set. Length: 10·5in (26·67cm).

4 Gauge "0" Four-Wheeled Electric P.O. E1.31 Locomotive by Hornby, France. These Bobigny-made 20-volt electric models, based on a type used on the Paris-Orleans-Midi Railway, were made from the early 1930s until World War II, and were reissued post-War in more

jazzy colours. The body pressings are among the most elaborate ever undertaken by French Hornby, with a wealth of detail that includes louvres, rivets and springs. The model was marketed for a time in Britain—see (8). The pre-War dark-green version shown here is fairly scarce; the brighter post-War versions are more common. Length: 8·25in (20·955cm).

5 Gauge "0" Four-Wheeled Goods Van, "DSB", by Hornby, Britain, issued in c1934-35. This vehicle, with hinged opening doors, is one of those lettered by Hornby in foreign liveries, in this case, the Danish State Railway. It must be remembered that Hornby exported many such items: they may be found in various European liveries and in those of South Africa, New

Zealand, South America, and the USA. They are unlikely to be found outside the countries for which they were intended, but most collectors would not go to great lengths to obtain such "oddballs". Length: 5·5in (13·97cm).

6 Gauge "0" Single-Barrel Wine Wagon. This rather garish wagon is by far the rarer of the wine wagons originated by French Hornby but issued in Britain in 1928-29. The double-barrelled version, with ladder and service platform but lacking the brake hut, is much easier to find: it replaced the single-barrelled version in the early 1930s, both items having for a while been issued concurrently. Length: 5·5in (13·97cm).

7 Gauge "0" No 2 Bogie Cattle Truck, "DSB"; another Hornby vehicle intended for Denmark—see (5). Like the No 2 Luggage Van, this was one of Hornby's earlier goods vehicles. It was available in form almost unchanged (except for liveries) from the 1920s until World War II, and is easy enough to find in British liveries. Length: 9in (22·86cm).

8 Gauge "0" No LEC1 Locomotive, numbered "10655" and lettered for Swiss Federal Railways, by Hornby, dating from the 1930s. This is a clockwork, reversing model, based on the P.O.E1 seen at (4); a 20-volt AC version, No LE1/20, was also available in Great Britain. Note that this version for the British market has done away with the dummy skirting, axle-boxes and springs of the French version shown at (4), evidently to suggest a Swiss appearance by leaving the wheels mostly exposed. Basically, this may be described as a French model of a Swiss type with a "Made in England" transfer! Length: 8·25in (20·955cm).

9 Gauge "0" Four-Wheeled "Wagons-Lits" Blue Pullman, by Hornby, France, mid-1930s. This odd little vehicle is probably French Hornby's version of the British company's M1 Pullman, although the vehicles differ in dimensions, and suggests some planning cooperation between the British and French companies. Length: 4·75in (12cm).

10 Gauge "0" Covered Wagon, "Nord"; a French-style vehicle by Hornby, issued in the mid-1930s. Based on the British No 1 version, this wagon was fitted with a tarpaulin on hoops (missing here). Quite a number of French-style vehicles, all lettered "Nord", were issued for the British market, but no French locomotive appropriate to these vehicles was ever put on the market. Length: 5·5in (13·97cm).

11 Gauge "0" Two-Car Diesel Articulated Set, electric, by Jep, France, available during the late 1930s and again after World War II. Although not a particularly inspiring model, it is characteristic of the little local trains so common in France and is very robustly made and quite well proportioned. It is fairly rare, although not avidly sought after by collectors. Length (overall): 12·25in (31·1cm).

1 Gauge "0" 4-4-4 Tank Locomotive, numbered "1534", by Hornby, Great Britain. This famous Hornby locomotive is shown here in its early form, dating from 1923, complete with its original box of embossed cardboard. It has a polished brass dome and is fitted with cast-iron wheels. This model, now most collectable and a "must" for Hornby enthusiasts, was made in clockwork only, and appeared in the liveries of the major British railway companies. The locomotive shown here is in the livery of the London and North Eastern Railway (L&NER; note that the ampersand marks this as an early example, since the form "LNER" was introduced in the early 1920s). As is the case with many Hornby items, examples in Southern Railway (SR) livery are hard to find. Length: 10·5in (26·67cm).

2 Gauge "0" 0-4-0 Tank Locomotive, numbered "623" and in London, Midland & Scottish Railway (LMS) livery, by Hornby. This is one of the rare permanent-magnet 6-volt No 1 locomotives, introduced in 1929, and is shown here in its original "Hornby Series" box, complete with its DC current forward-and-reverse speed controller. It is interesting to note that the Meccano company never took DC locomotives very seriously and later concentrated on AC current locomotives with elaborate reversing gear. This very attractive tank engine was produced in the colours of the four major British railway companies, and in "goods black". Length: 7in (17·78cm).

3 Gauge "0" 0-4-0 No 1 Tank Locomotive, in Great Western Railway (GWR) livery, by Hornby; one of the firm's earliest production models, appearing in the early 1920s. Early examples are of bolted construction, but the more usual tabbed assembly was later adopted. The model underwent some refinement in the late 1920s, and a version was produced bearing the name "Zulu". A tender variety—see (8)—was also made available. The locomotive was made in the major British and many continental liveries. The example shown is clockwork, with the usual brake and forward/reverse control knobs protruding from the rear of the cab: it was later made in electric versions, and most collectors find the 6-volt electric

model much more attractive than its EPM16 successor. Length: 6·5in (16·51cm).

4 Gauge "0" Snow Plough, lettered "Snow Plough" and in GWR colours; an early mid-series Hornby item. Especially heavy wheels were fitted to this model, and a spring belt ran around a V-pulley on the leading axle to drive the Meccano fan, or "snow pusher". The cast lamp above the fan appears only on the earlier versions; nor do the sliding doors feature on later models. The snow plough was made in many different colour schemes, finally appearing in bright yellow and blue—see (12), *pages 90-91*, for a late version. Length (with plough): 7in (17·78cm).

5 Gauge "0" Private Owner Van, "Carr's Biscuits", by Hornby;

an early version with a spindly chassis and link couplings. Note that these early vans are fitted with hinged, opening doors; later versions have sliding doors. It is interesting to compare the "Hornby Series" rectangle on this van's solebar with the later version seen on the control unit at (2). Length: 5·5in (13·97cm).

6-7 Gauge "0" Four-Wheeled Coach, Third Class (6), and Guard's Van (7), by Hornby, dating from the late 1920s. Note that these coaches have clerestory roofs: on later coaches, elliptical roofs were fitted, but removal of these will reveal the turned-over end of the earlier clerestory versions. These coaches were available in the four major British liveries: the examples shown are in LMS colours and,

again, SR versions are the hardest to find. Length: 6in (15·24cm).

8 Gauge "0" 0-4-0 No 1 Tender Locomotive, with Four-Wheeled Tender numbered "2710", clockwork, by Hornby; one of the earliest production models—see also (3). A non-reversing version with an identical body was also available. Later versions had longer splashers and had tenders that were lettered for the railway companies rather than with the number "2710". This example is in the livery of the London and North Eastern Railway (LNER); note the characteristic Hornby "Forward" crest on the cab side, and the Hornby "garter" behind the polished dome (a little shabby on this "play-worn" example). Length (engine and tender): 10·25in (26·035cm).

On this spread are shown Hornby locomotives of the type generally known as "Number 3", denoting 4-4-2 locomotives of a type initiated at the Meccano factory at Bobigny, France. It is thought that, after production of the initial "Nord" French locomotive for the "Blue Train"—see (1)—Hornby of Britain decided to use the French body-pressings, with minor modifications, for locomotives in the liveries of the four major British railways. Early models in the series retained typically French "stove-pipe" funnels, but these were soon replaced by a more British equivalent. In the caes of all the locomotives shown here, it would appear that the locomotive body pressings only were of French origin; in fact, it is possible that it was only the body press-tools that were shipped from Bobigny to Liverpool, rather than great quantities of unpainted body casings.

1 Gauge "0" E320 4-4-2 "Riviera Blue" Locomotive and Eight-Wheeled Tender, both numbered "3.1290" and in "Nord" finish. This is one of the last of the long run, a 20-volt electric model in the matt finish of the immediate pre-War period, with the improved tender bogies and characteristic smoke deflectors of the later examples. This style of locomotive probably underwent more changes and colour variations than any other Hornby item. Representing the famous "Blue Train" that ran from Calais to the Riviera via Paris, it was originated by Hornby of France but was also very popular in Britain. The locomotive first appeared in 1926, in clockwork or 4-volt electric, and then had a polished brass boiler dome, a fixed headlamp, and smaller driving wheels made of cast-iron. The 1930s saw models in 6-volt electric, No 2 Special clockwork and, later still, No 2 20-volt automatic reversing motors. The polished domes soon disappeared in favour of black- or brown-painted versions, and the smoke deflectors were added around 1936. Many different numbers were used—it is now not unusual to find specimens with non-matching tender numbers —and Hornby, France, produced these locomotives in most French railway liveries, some highly inappropriate. They are not too difficult to find in one form or another and are a most important feature of any Hornby collection. Note that a locomotive of French origin will display on its tender-mounted gold rectangle: "Série Hornby/Fab. par/ Meccano, Paris"; the British model will have: "Made in England/by/ Meccano Ltd./Hornby Series". Length: (engine and tender): 16·5in (41·91cm).

2 Gauge "0" E320 4-4-2 "Lord Nelson" Locomotive and Six-Wheeled Tender, numbered "850" and in Southern Railway (SR) colours. The example shown is a late model in 20-volt electric. Earlier models

in the series, made before 1930, had a tender quite different from that seen here: the early No 2 tender, as for the type "2711", with distinctive coal rails around the top. These were superseded by the far more elaborate and accurately-detailed tender seen here. But both the earlier and later tenders were also sold as separate items, to suit the numbering of the locomotives; thus, the finish seen here might also feature on an earlier tender. "Lord Nelson" is one of the rarer names in the series; pre-1930 versions are very rare, although mid-1930s examples are not too difficult to find. Length (engine and tender): 16in (40·64cm).

3 Gauge "0" E320 4-4-2 "Royal Scot" Locomotive, numbered "6100", and Six-Wheeled Tender, in London, Midland & Scottish Railway (LMS) livery; a late 1930s version in 20-volt electric. Both "Royal Scot" and "Flying Scotsman" (5) were made in great numbers in clockwork and electric: the famous names alone must have sold these models, which are not at all true-to-prototype. The earlier French-influenced version was interesting in that it had the "6100" number on the tender, the cab side bearing a large, round LMS coat-of-arms. It may be that "red" locomotives had the greatest appeal, since significantly more examples were sold in LMS colours than any other. LMS colours were also chosen for such markets as India and South Africa, although the name was then deleted and the appropriate railway companies' initials replaced "LMS". These models are not at all rare, although a mint specimen is most collectable. Length (engine and tender): 16in (40·64cm).

4 Gauge "0" E320 4-4-2 "Caerphilly Castle" Locomotive, numbered "4073", and Six-Wheeled Tender, in Great Western Railway (GWR) colours. This 20-volt electric version displays three minor modifications when compared to other locomotives of the same series at (3) and (5). A somewhat larger chimney has replaced the earlier "stove-pipe"; a strange-looking brass version of the typical GWR safety-valve is fitted halfway along the boiler; and the usual French-type safety-valve immediately in front of the cab has been replaced by a brass whistle. "Caerphilly Castle" is slightly rarer than "Royal Scot" or "Flying Scotsman". Length (engine and tender): 16in (40·64cm).

5 Gauge "0" E320 4-4-2 "Flying Scotsman" Locomotive, numbered "4472", and Six-Wheeled Tender, in 20-volt electric, by Hornby. It can be said that this model looks even less like the locomotive whose name it bears than any other in the series: save for its name, number, and its London and North Eastern Railway (LNER) livery, it has no features in common with its prototype. An extremely popular model, it remains easy to find. Length (engine and tender): 16in (40·64cm).

1-4 Gauge "0" No 1 0-4-0 Tank Locomotive, numbered "667", in Southern Railway (SR) colours. This Hornby locomotive of the late 1920s, available in the liveries of the major British railway companies, is shown here hauling a train of contemporary Hornby goods vehicles: "Colman's Mustard" Van (2); "Seccotine Sticks Everything" Van (3); and "United Dairies" Milk Tank Wagon (4). The locomotive shown here is clockwork, with brake and reversing gear: it is quite a scarce item in this form, but is much rarer in the later 6-volt electric version. Note the characteristically large handrails and knobs, the fixed dummy front lamps, and the over-height buffer level. The wheels of these early Hornby locomotives

are of lead-alloy, or cast-iron in some of the larger models, so they are not liable to the fatigue often encountered in the mazac (zinc-alloy) wheels of some later models. Of the rolling stock in this train, "Colman's Mustard" is probably the rarest of all Hornby vans, and "Seccotine" the next rarest. On "Seccotine", note Hornby's advertising rectangle to the right of the sole-bar, and compare this typical mark of the later 1920s with the earlier "Meccano" oval on the "Shell" tank wagon at (7). The "United Dairies" milk tank wagon is perhaps the most popular model of its type. Note that all three vehicles are of the earlier type, dating from before c1931, with open chassis and link couplings.

Lengths (locomotive: 6·5in (16·51cm); (each wagon): 5·5in (13·97cm).

5 Gauge "0" No 0 Clockwork Tender Locomotive, 0-4-0, and Four-Wheeled Tender, numbered "2710", in Great Western Railway (GWR) colours. A very early Hornby series, issued in the early 1920s, in non-reversing clockwork with brake, these locomotives were produced with various changes up to the early 1930s. The number "2710" marks the earlier production run. This was priced in the 1930s at 10s 6d (52½p, 63c), the tender being 2s 6d (12½p, 15c) extra, and, as in some cheaper models, the hand-rail knobs were diecast, the entire hand-rail assembly being painted gold. Length (engine and tender): 10·5in (26·67cm).

6 Gauge "0" Open Wagon, Hornby, 1920s. This is the earliest form of Hornby's open wagon, of bolted construction, with blank axle-guards, turned-brass buffers and brass link couplings, and with the letters "LNWR" (London and North-Western Railway) individually pressed and clipped on. Length: 5·5in (13·97cm).

7 Gauge "0" Tank Wagon, "Shell", Hornby, 1920s. Hornby produced many private owner tank wagons based on this very early version, with its plain axle-guards and locomotive-valve-style filler. As in (6), its underside bears the early press-stamped marking "MLDL (the "D" superimposed above the horizontal stroke of the first "L"), England" ("Meccano Limited, Liverpool, England"). This is a rare item.

Length: 5·5in (13·97cm).

8 Gauge "0" No 2 Corridor Coach, LNER, Hornby, 1930s. This is one of a series that appeared in the four major liveries as both coaches and brake ends. Somewhat under-scale, they represent the maker's first attempt to break away from all-Pullman mainline trains, and illustrate also the use of lithographed tinplate to keep down cost. Note "The Queen of Scots" title-board (which properly belongs on an LNER Pullman): most Hornby corridor coaches of the 1930s were provided with brackets to hold destination- or title-boards, which were available in great variety as separate items. Length: 11·75in (29·845cm).

9 Gauge "0" No 2 Special 4-4-0 Locomotive, "Yorkshire", and Six-Wheeled Tender, numbered "234", in LNER livery. This was the first of the famous No 2 Special Locomotives which appeared around 1929. For a fuller account of this series see *pages 92-93,* where the later version of this locomotive, "Bramham Moor", is shown at (4). This example can be distinguished as one of the first series by the fact that the number "234" and letters "LNER" both appear on the tender side: on later models, "234" appears on the cab side. Length: 14·625in (37·15cm).

10 Gauge "0" Metropolitan Brake Coach, Hornby, 1920s. This brake coach, and a matching passenger coach, was issued to complement the Metropolitan Electric locomotive shown at (11); the items were boxed in sets from the outset. A well-lithographed representation of its prototype, it features an intriguing interior lighting system via brass roller-pickups to the track. All Metropolitan coach roofs are fitted with the knurled nut system, and this coach always retained the early, rigid, pressed bogie, although compensated bogies were fitted to other coaches. Length: 13in (33·02cm).

11 Gauge "0" Metropolitan Electric Locomotive; this item was first issued by Hornby in *c*1926 as a high-voltage model running at 110 volts AC, the controller being in series with a 60-watt lamp. This system was obviously dangerous—indeed, it is thought that the British authorities planned to legislate against it!—and a 4-volt version to work off an accumulator soon appeared, along with a clockwork version. In the 1930s the model was classified as "Series 3", and improved 6-volt and, finally, 20-volt automatic reversing versions appeared. Production ended in 1939. The all-lithographed body is a well-proportioned representation of a prototype used on London's Metropolitan Railway at the time of the Wembley Exhibition of 1926, but so far as the wheel arrangement is concerned, this model of a BO-BO electric locomotive is, in fact, an 0-4-0 disguised by a pressed skirt, making it rather unconvincing if viewed at track level. It is a most collectable item in any form. Length: 9·7in (24·765cm).

1 Gauge "0" No 2 Corridor Coach (Brake Composite), Great Western Railway (GWR), issued by Hornby in 1937. With this series, Hornby attempted to break away from its familiar saloons: the vehicle represents a modification in tooling and is based on the earlier non-corridor passenger coaches but with new artwork. Hornby allowed the lithography to reveal the brightly tinned finish of the window areas, and in these areas of simulated glazing the vehicle is at its most vulnerable: with aging, the thin protective lacquer wears away from the silvering, which takes on a decidedly dull appearance. This effect should not be confused with the attempts at shading visible in the excellent example shown here.

Along with its Southern Railway (SR) counterpart, this coach has an important place in the affections of Hornby collectors: examples with good lithography are highly prized, and in good condition they are very rare. Length: 11.5in (29.21cm).

2 Gauge "0" No 2 Saloon Coach in London, Midland & Scottish Railway (LMS) livery. Available also in London and North Eastern Railway (LNER) livery, this somewhat uninspired Hornby vehicle had a long run, following on from the similar 1920s version shown at (9) and available in various forms from the early 1930s until World War II. It is difficult to understand why a vehicle so lacking in important detail remained in production

for so long. It has gelatine windows with printed table-lamps, like the far superior No 2 Special Pullman, and one may say in its favour that it is extremely well made of heavy-gauge tinplate —which explains why so many examples survive, making this an easily-obtainable item. Length: 12.75in (32.385cm).

3 Gauge "0" Four-Wheeled Midland Railway Coach. This little vehicle, although of somewhat crude appearance, nicely illustrates Hornby's production in the earlier 1920s. As in many other vehicles of the period, the coach body is bolted to the chassis; the numbers "1" and "3" are separate brass pressings clipped to the door sides. Note the fine Midland coat-of-arms.

These coaches were issued to complement some of the early all-bolted No 1-type locomotives; no brake versions were made. They are quite scarce in any livery. Length: 5.5in (13.97cm).

4 Gauge "0" No 2 Corridor Coach (Brake Composite), SR; in this livery, the most desirable of the range described at (1). Notice that these coaches, like the No 2 Special Pullmans, were provided with brackets, either on the roof, as seen here, or at the sides in the LMS version, to carry a wide range of train titles and destinations. In the early 1930s these roof/side boards were of blue card with gold lettering. Tinplate versions in blue and gold soon took over and then, as seen here, more realistic black

lettering on white tinplate boards
was adopted by the maker.
Length: 11·5in (29·21cm).
5 Gauge "0" Guard's Van, SR
(also available in LMS, LNER,
and GWR colours), issued in the
mid-to-late 1930s as the companion
to Hornby's No 1 Passenger Coach.
A pleasing foreshortened version
of the No 2 Bogie Passenger Coach,
this vehicle was reissued after
World War II, with a British
Railways (BR) version at the end
of the run. The SR and GWR
versions are by far the hardest
to find. Length: 6·25in (15·875cm).
6 Gauge "0" Passenger Coach,
LMS, issued by Hornby in 1927.
The late 1920's versions, as seen,
had clerestory roofs; modification
in the early 1930s resulted in
non-clerestory, or elliptical,

roofs. The early type appeared
also in LNER and GWR colours,
but it was not until after
modification that an SR version
was produced—see (7). Oddly,
these little coaches, including a
Brake Van, see (11), complemented
Hornby's large 4-4-4 tank
locomotive in sets of four; more
appropriately, they accompanied
the No 1 "2710" locomotives.
Length: 6in (15·24cm).
7 Gauge "0" Passenger Coach,
SR; the modification noted at
(6). Note the early type chassis,
always used in these vehicles,
which now has a fold to
represent side footboards; the
reduced buffer height; the
automatic couplings; and the
opening doors. SR versions are
comparatively very rare.

Length: 6in (15·24cm).
8 Gauge "0" No 2 Corridor Coach
(Brake Composite), LMS. With its
companion Corridor Coach, this
LMS version is by far the most
common of the No 2 Corridor
Coaches. Really good examples,
however, are valued by collectors.
Length: 11·5in (29·21cm).
9 Gauge "0" Dining Saloon; the
earliest Hornby vehicle, dating
from c1924. It is almost entirely
of bolted construction and has
axles similar to Meccano rods.
One wonders where Hornby found
this livery of green and ivory
with grey-green roof—and further
to confuse the issue the coach
bears a fine Midland Railway
coat-of-arms. A companion coach
was lettered "Pullman", and
later these vehicles were produced

in the familiar Pullman umber-
and-cream colours. These early
vehicles are fairly scarce in good
condition, but a surprising
number have survived. Length:
12·75in (32·385cm).
10 Gauge "0" Passenger Coach,
GWR. As noted at (6) and (7),
these little vehicles mark the
transitional period from Hornby's
early "toy-like" approach to a
rather more sophisticated look.
Length: 6in (15·24cm).
11 Gauge "0" Guard's Van, the
companion to (10), in GWR
passenger livery. Although the
clerestory roof has been dropped,
sliding back the top will reveal
the turned-over ends of the earlier
clerestory version. The vehicles
of this series should not be hard
to find. Length: 6in (15·24cm).

The collecting hobby may be pursued in many different ways, and some toy train collectors will choose to specialize in one aspect only of the wide range open to them. As shown here, a collection of Hornby tank wagons, with their many variations, would certainly make a good show. Generally speaking, wagons are among the easiest Hornby items to collect, although some have now achieved parity in desirability—and in value—with certain Hornby locomotives. Seen here is a good selection of tank wagons produced by Hornby from the 1920s until World War II. Al the wagons shown on this spread are in Gauge "0", and all are of the same length (measured over buffers): 5·625in (14·29cm).

1 Milk Tank Wagon, "Nestlés Milk", in production from the mid-1930s until World War II. This wagon succeeded the "United Dairies" model shown at (3); both have the late-type chassis and automatic couplings, but "United Dairies" is also to be found with the early chassis and couplings, as shown at (4).
2 Bitumen Tank Wagon, "Colas", available up to World War II. The model is similar to (1), but lacks a ladder. The "Colas" wagon in red, as seen, is quite rare; the earlier blue one is more common.
3 Milk Tank Wagon, "United Dairies"; a high-quality model of the early 1930s. Dating between the earlier "United Dairies" (4) and the "Nestlés Milk" wagon (1), this is a little rarer than other

milk tank wagons; it has the late chassis and automatic couplings, and chassis and trimmings are finished in blue.
4 Milk Tank Wagon, "United Dairies"; late 1920s. This is the earlier model: note the early-type chassis with open axle-guards, link couplings, and the grey finish of chassis and trimmings. These early Hornby wagons have a higher, over-scale buffer height.
5 Petrol Tank Wagon, "Pratts"; a standard tank wagon of the early 1930s, with the later pressed chassis and automatic couplings. This is not hard to find.
6 Petrol Tank Wagon, "Esso"; an example from the late 1930s, not particularly rare, in which the nicely-detailed cast tank filler top seen on (5) and on other earlier

models on this spread has been replaced by one embossed in the tinplate dome.
7 Petrol Tank Wagon No 1, "Power Ethyl"; another late model, but one of the most attractive in the series, and not so easy to find. Note that this example is wrongly fitted with link couplings; they should be automatic.
8 Petrol Tank Wagon No 1, "Pool"; the last of the pre-War run. "Pool" petrol, replacing the familiar named brands, was introduced as a wartime measure, which suggests that production of this wagon extended into the early stages of World War II.
9 Motor Spirit Tank Wagon, "National Benzole"; one of the early series, dating from the 1920s, with the early chassis and

large-link couplings. Note that the tank ends had a considerably greater return than on later models. Not too hard to find.

10 Petrol Tank Wagon, "Redline-Glico"; one of the first austere-detail tank wagons, lacking the cast filler top, of the early 1930s. It is not hard to find; see also (18).

11 Petrol Tank Wagon, "Shell"; one of the most common tank wagons, available from the mid-1930s until World War II. This example is one of the non-buffered versions that were used in certain Hornby "M Series" sets.

12 Petrol Tank Wagon "BP". This had a long run for one of the less colourful items, and may be found with either link or automatic couplings. Good examples of this

wagon are fairly common.

13 Petrol Tank Wagon, "Pratts". A yellow-ochre finish replaced the earlier green—see (14)—in this model of the early 1930s, but the lettering layout remained almost identical. Although having the later pressed chassis, this wagon is still fitted with link couplings and probably marks the transitional period. It is less easy to find than (14).

14 Petrol Tank Wagon, "Pratts"; the earlier green version, dating from the 1920s. This wagon had a reasonably long production run and is easier to find than the later version shown at (13).

15 Oil Tank Wagon, "Mobiloil"; one of the last series, dating from 1939-40, and with the austere top. It is interesting to note

that Hornby never truly established a standard location for its own advertising rectangle. It appears on this and most other later items at one end, where it does not affect the side lettering, but on earlier models—for example, (3), (5), and (12)—its position varies. This model is not one of the easiest of the Hornby wagons for the collector to find.

16 Petrol Tank Wagon, "BP". This model of the mid-1930s retains the cast filler top into the period of the late chassis and automatic couplings; it may prove to be rather harder to find than some others in the series.

17 Oil Tank Wagon, "Castrol"; a rather poor example of a mid-1930s Hornby wagon that is still easy to find.

18 Petrol Tank Wagon, "Redline"; the predecessor of (10), dating from the early 1930s. As seen here, with automatic couplings, this wagon seems to be rather harder to find that the earlier version with open chassis and with large-link couplings.

19 Oil Tank Wagon, "Royal Daylight", dating from the later 1930s. This is one of the most common of Hornby's pre-War tank wagons: the collector should only accept a good example and should not bother with the purchase and subsequent restoration of one in poor condition.

20 Petrol Tank Wagon No 1 "Motor Spirit" ("Shell" and "BP"); one of the most attractive of the late series, this tank wagon is comparatively rare.

On this spread, and elsewhere in this book, the terms "printed" or "lithographed", or "painted and transferred", are often used to indicate the finish of items. In "lithographed/printed" items, all the model is printed in flat sheet tinplate, giving maximum artwork effect but limiting detail pressing. In "painted and transferred" items, the bodywork of the model is pressed to incorporate such detail as planking, etc, and is then spray-painted and hand-transferred. The latter process, although more expensive, results in a less realistic appearance.

All the vehicles shown on this spread are of the same length (measured over the buffers): 5·625in (14·29cm).

1 Gauge "0" No 0 Fish Van by Hornby, Great Britain, lithographed for the London, Midland & Scottish Railway (LMS). Available only from the later 1930s until World War II — and catalogued by Hornby at a price of 1s 6d (7½p, 9c) in 1939 — this rather attractive van is now quite scarce.

2 Gauge "0" No 0 Refrigerator Van, lithographed for the LMS. Like (1), with the same history and price, this model is quite realistically printed to incorporate all necessary body detail. Although lithographed items are cheaper than painted and transferred ones, they seem more convincing when judged simply as models. This van is not very easy to find.

3 Gauge "0" No 0 Refrigerator Van, lithographed for the Southern Railway (SR); otherwise as (2). These refrigerator vans were available in the four major British liveries: the "SR" version is the most difficult to find; in fact, one might find twenty "LMS" for every one "SR".

4 Gauge "0" No 0 Fish Van, lithographed for the Great Western Railway (GWR); otherwise as (1). It was also available as "LMS" (1) and "NE" (5), but the "GW" version is quite hard for the collector to find.

5 Gauge "0" No 0 Fish Van, lithographed in the standard goods vehicle colours of the London and North Eastern Railway (LNER). More attractive than the dark-brown "GW" version at (4),

this van seems easier to find than those at (1) and (4).

6 Gauge "0" Brake Van, single-ended and with opening doors, painted and transferred for the GWR: one of the more expensively finished items, priced at 2s 9d (13½p, 16c) in the late 1930s. These vehicles, also available in "LMS", enjoyed a long run, from the beginnings of Hornby's activities in the 1920s until World War II, and they are among the easiest of all Hornby goods vehicles to find. There are a number of variations in both the single-end version, seen here, and the double-ended "SR" or "NE" version, shown at (7). Examples from the early 1920s are bolted to the chassis and have very large couplings and

brightly-plated tinplate wheels. Later vans will be found with the early chassis with small link couplings, and with the late chassis with automatic couplings. There are striking colour variations also, including giant red-shaded gold lettering, and bright green chassis and roof.

7 Gauge "0" Brake Van, double-ended and with opening doors, painted and transferred "SR", and also available "NE". Athough both single- and double-ended brake vans are fairly common, the "SR" version may be a little harder to find. The double-ended van reappeared in the 1940s in "NE" and "BR" (British Railways) versions only.

8 Gauge "0" No 0 Refrigerator Van, lithographed for the LNER;

otherwise details are as (2).

9 Gauge "0" No 0 Milk Traffic Van, lithographed for the GWR and available only in this finish, in brown with yellow lettering, from the later 1930s. This vehicle, which is quite common, superseded a mid-1930s version that had a grey litho-graphed body and sliding doors.

10 Gauge "0" Coal Wagon, a painted and transferred model, catalogued at 2s 3d (11p, 13c) in c1937. This is similar to the Hornby No 1 Wagon, but is found with the lettering "Hornby Railway Company", as shown, or "Meccano", and is fitted with an embossed coal top. An attractive and much sought after item that might be described as Hornby's own "private owner" wagon.

11 Gauge "0" "Cadbury's Chocolates" Van, painted and transferred, with sliding doors, and available from the early 1930s until World War II. A handsome vehicle, available in two styles of lettering, this is not so scarce as some other private owner vehicles.

12 Gauge "0" No 1 Banana Van, "Fyffes", painted and transferred, with sliding doors. Introduced in the early 1930s, this is the most common of the private owner vans. It is found in shades of yellow and green with white roof, or, as seen here, in yellow and red, with red roof. Early versions had outward-opening doors.

13 Gauge "0" Sausage Van, "Palethorpes", painted and transferred, with sliding doors.

This attractive vehicle was a relative latecomer to the range in the later 1930s. It is fairly rare and much sought after.

14 Gauge "0" "Crawford's Biscuits" Van, painted and transferred. This model was available from the late 1920s until World War II, undergoing the usual changes of chassis and couplings—see (6)—and from hinged to sliding doors. Earlier versions have white roofs; later ones red. It is a relatively common item in the private owner series. It is believed that Meccano came to an arrangement whereby companies whose names appeared on Hornby private owner vehicles met the expenses involved and also paid a small royalty to the maker.

1 Gauge "0" E120 Special Electric 0-4-0 Locomotive and Four-Wheeled Tender, numbered "179", by Hornby, Great Britain. This No 1 Special locomotive was first available in clockwork in 1929; the electric version seen here appeared in the early 1930s, and production continued until World War II. The example shown is one of the de luxe 0-4-0s, a desirable item for Hornby collectors. It was available in the liveries of the four major British companies: the Southern Railway (SR) version shown here seems to be by far the scarcest. With apparent design affinity to the Hornby No 2 Special 4-4-0 "Yorkshire"/"Bramham Moor", this locomotive was quite highly priced: in 1937 it was catalogued at £1 7s 6d (£1.37½,

$1.65) in electric, or 15s 9d (78½p, 94c) in clockwork; the tender being 3s 3d (16p, 19c) extra in either version. The locomotive was also boxed with three four-wheeled coaches in exotic-sounding passenger sets: "Comet" for the LMS; "Queen of Scots' for the LNER; "Torbay Express' for the GWR; and "Bournemouth Belle" for the SR, as shown here (less one Pullman) at (1-3.) Length (engine and tender): 11·75in (29·845cm).
2-3 Gauge "0" No 1 Pullman Coach (2), "Cynthia", also available as "Corsair"; and Pullman Coach Composite (3), "Ansonia", also available as "Aurora". These small vehicles were issued by Hornby in sets with the No 1 Special tender-type locomotive (1). Earlier versions have opening end and

baggage doors and are fitted with link couplings. Desirable for the Hornby collector, they are not rare. Length: 6·625in (16·83cm).
4 Gauge "0" Type 101 0-4-0 Tank Locomotive, numbered "2270", by Hornby, c1954. This locomotive can only be distinguished from its pre-War counterpart by the style of its "Hornby" label (not visible here) and the size of its funnel (smaller in the pre-War version). Pre-War locomotives should also have bright-red wheels. It was made in clockwork, as seen, and electric versions and appeared in the four major liveries—the SR and GWR versions being the scarcer—and finally in British Railways (BR) black. Electric models are harder to find than clockwork ones, but none of the

series should be difficult to come by. Length: 6·5in (16·51cm).
5-6 Gauge "0" Four-Wheeled Coaches, in London and North-Western Railway (L&NWR) livery; these are early Hornby vehicles, dating from around 1924. At this time, vehicles bore no "Hornby" label; instead, the undersides are marked with the letters "MLLD" (the "D" being superimposed on the horizontal of the first "L") above the word "England"—signifying "Meccano Limited, Liverpool, England". These early items are hard to find. Length: 5·5in (13·97cm).
7 Gauge "0" No 1 0-4-0 Locomotive and Four-Wheeled Tender, numbered "2710". This clockwork model is another early Hornby item, first issued in the 1920s in a fairly plain form. The example

shown is in LMS colours; they appeared in various liveries but no SR version was made and examples in GWR or Caledonian Railway blue liveries are rarer than others. However, examples of this reasonably collectable locomotive should not be too hard to find. Length (engine and tender): 10·5in (26·67cm).

8 Gauge "0" M1 0-4-0 Locomotive and Four-Wheeled Tender, numbered "3435", made by Hornby from the early 1930s until World War II and again post-War. This little clockwork, reversing locomotive was catalogued at 4s 6d (22½p, 27c) in 1937, with the tender 9d (3½p, 4c) extra. In its red and bright-green versions it was sold in great quantity and should be easy to find. Some pre-War colours may

be more difficult to acquire, and 6-volt and 20-volt electric models are the scarcest of all. Post-War production—all clockwork, like all post-1945 Hornby Gauge "0" models—included a much-altered version in BR colours. Length (engine and tender): 9in (22·86cm).
9-10 Gauge "0" M1 Pullman Coaches, "Marjorie" (9) and "Aurelia" (10), also found as "Viking", made by Hornby from the early 1930s to complement, among other models, the M1 locomotive (8). These are among the most common Hornby coaches: they were marketed in many boxed sets and were available separately at a price, in 1937, of 1s 0d (5p, 6c) each. Length: 4·75in (12·065cm).
11 Gauge "0" E120 Special Electric 0-40 Tank Locomotive, numbered

"5500". This Hornby model was made in clockwork from 1929 until World War II, the electric version appearing in c1934. The companion to the No 1 Special Tender locomotive at (1), this was available in the four major liveries: the GWR version is shown here. This tank engine seems to be far more common than the tender variety, even in SR colours, but, as with most Hornby locomotives, electric models are far scarcer than clockwork: for every ten clockwork models, the collector may only encounter one electric specimen. In any form, it is an important addition to a Hornby collection. Length: 7·125in (18·097cm).
12-14 Gauge "0" 0-4-0 Locomotive and Four-Wheeled Tender (14), numbered "6161", with M0 Pullman

Coaches, "Joan" (12) and "Zena" (13). This little set, made in non-reversing clockwork only, was introduced by Hornby in the early 1930s and reappeared after World War II. The passenger set was priced in 1933 at 5s 9d (28½p, 34c). Unlike the post-War example seen here, the earlier locomotive had no cylinders or motion (side-rods). Pre-War versions, in which a fixed key appeared, were numbered "4472" in green or "6100" in red. Post-War versions continued into a more convincing BR passenger livery. As well as coaches, some wagons were made to complement the locomotive. Apart from the earliest versions, all components of this set are fairly easy to find. Lengths (engine and tender): 8·5in (21·59cm); (coach): 4in (10·16cm).

1 Gauge "0" No 2 High Capacity Wagon, in London and North Eastern Railway colours, by Hornby, Great Britain. In the later 1930s, Hornby produced a very convincing series of bogie high capacity wagons—see also (8)—including this brick transport version. As seen, rather over-sized wooden bricks were made as a load. These all-lithographed vehicles are perhaps slightly better-looking than their Winteringham/Bassett-Lowke counterparts, but were lower priced: 3s 9d (18½p, 22c) each in 1937. Many of these handsome vehicles have survived and they are fairly easy to find. Length: 11·75in (29·845cm).

2 Gauge "0" Trolley Wagon with Cable Drums; a vehicle with a long production run, introduced by Hornby in the mid-to-late 1920s and continuing with little change other than in liveries—but see also note at (6)—until World War II. In 1938, it was priced at 4s 3d (21p, 25c) with cable drums, or 3s 9d (18½p, 22c) without. It is fairly easy to find. Length: 12·75in (32·385cm).

3 Gauge "0" Gas Cylinder Wagon; a rather uninspiring vehicle and another long-lived one, with a production run extending from the mid-1920s until World War II, and reissued thereafter until the 1960s. Earlier versions, with open chassis, are more interesting: they have separately-applied black straps and the cylinders are lettered for the four major railway companies. Otherwise, this is not an item of great interest.

Length: 5·5in (13·97cm).

4 Gauge "0" No 2 Timber Wagon: one of Hornby's earliest vehicles and in production until World War II. This somewhat gaunt bogie wagon is very easy to find. Length: 12·5in (31·75cm).

5 Gauge "0" No 1 Crane Truck, first issued by Hornby in the mid-1920s and produced up to and after World War II. Its play-value—the crane swivels and the hook can be manually raised and lowered—made it a popular toy, but it is of no great value to the collector. Length: 5·5in (13·97cm).

6 Gauge "0" No 1 Rotary Tipping Wagon; made by Hornby from the mid-1920s onward and reappearing post-War. Like the other vehicles with a long production run, it underwent design changes: before

c1931, open chassis and link couplings were usual; after that date, a more embossed and detailed chassis was used, generally with automatic couplings. As in many Hornby vehicles of the period, the colour scheme is rather garish. This wagon is fairly easy to find, although examples with "Meccano" or "Hornby" advertising are scarcer than the "Trinidad Lake Asphalt" version. Length: 5·5in (13·97cm).

7 Gauge "0" No 1 Side Tipping Wagon; production history as (6) —a mid-to-late period vehicle is shown here: as with many Hornby items, the earlier versions are rather more interesting. This is one of the more common Hornby wagons, although "Sir Robert MacAlpine" advertising versions are more usual than the "Robert

Hudson Ltd" example shown here. Length: 5·5in (13·97cm).

8 Gauge "0" No 2 High Capacity Wagon; another of the handsome, lithographed bogie open wagons as seen at (1) – but this one is the locomotive coal transport version lettered for the LMS. Judging by the numbers still available, a vast quantity of these wagons must have been produced up to World War II: a good example should be quite easy for the collector to find. Length: 11·75in (29·845cm).

9 Gauge "0" Flat Truck with Container, in Southern Railway (SR) colours; a Hornby vehicle of the mid-to-late 1930s. This appeared until World War II in the four major liveries – the SR version shown here may be the hardest to find – and reappeared post-War in

LMS, LNER, and British Railways (BR) versions only. The container is made of wood, with lithographed paper detail stuck on. Length: 5·5in (13·97cm).

10 Gauge "0" Flat Truck with Furniture Container; the LNER version of (9), identical to it in all respects save the livery and the detail of the container. Length: 5·5in (13·97cm).

11 Gauge "0" Cement Wagon; another Hornby vehicle with a long life, produced from the mid-1920s up to and after World War II. The usual version is the "Portland Cement" wagon in yellow, but the red one shown here is also fairly common. Earlier versions appeared in a rather more austere grey finish, again with gold lettering. Length: 5·5in (13·97cm).

12 Gauge "0" Snow Plough – see also (4), pages 76-77. The example shown here is one of the latest of Hornby's pre-War production run: the sliding doors and splendid cast searchlight of the earlier version are missing, and a garish colour scheme typical of Hornby in the later 1930s has been adopted. Obviously with a high play-value, this was a very popular toy. Length: 6·75in (17·145cm).

13 Gauge "0" No 1 Wagon; this model, catalogued at 1s 6d (7½p, 9c) in 1937, was the most convincing in appearance of Hornby's four-wheeled open wagons: on this model alone, Hornby added a printed solebar between the wagon body and the lower chassis, thus providing detail in what was otherwise an uninteresting area.

The wagon was lettered for the SR, as seen here, LMS, GWR and NE (the usual marking for LNER goods vehicles). Surprisingly close in quality to their more expensive Bassett-Lowke counterparts, these wagons, although by no means rare, are a welcome addition to a Hornby collection. Length: 5·5in (13·97cm).

14 Gauge "0" No 1 Wagon; as (13), but lettered for the LNER and fitted with the tarpaulin that was available as a separate item at a price, around 1937, of 2d (1p, 1c). It is surprising what added realism the tarpaulin, or a load of some kind, imparts to an open wagon. Although the wagon is easy enough to find, the tarpaulin may prove to be rather more elusive. Length: 5·5in (13·97cm).

With the exception of (5), the Hornby locomotives shown here belong to the No 2 Special series of express passenger trains which first appeared around 1929, representing Hornby's first attempts at near-scale modelling. They are well-made and finely-proportioned representations of 4-4-0 locomotives in the liveries of the four major British railway companies of the time. They continued in production, with minor changes, until World War II, but, like most of Hornby's better Gauge "0" models, did not reappear thereafter. They were originally available in clockwork, appearing in electric versions, as shown here, from around 1934. It should be noted that none of the locomotives shown here has

the smokebox headlamp that, in the opinion of many collectors, disfigured these otherwise pleasing models in their electric versions. The locomotives were made in the style shown for one year only: sales fell, and the ugly headlamp was restored—but the locomotives remained available without headlamp to special order. Hornby No 2 Special locomotives are not too difficult for the collector to find, although they are very scarce in good condition. They were popular toys, and most surviving examples have been well "play-worn". They would grace any general collection and are a "must" for the Hornby specialist.

1 Gauge "0", Hornby No 2 Special, 4-4-0 Standard Compound Loco-

motive, numbered "1185", and Six-Wheeled Tender, London, Midland & Scottish Railway (LMS); 20-volt electric. Like the other No 2 Special locomotives shown here, this model formed part of an express passenger train set—for full details of set make-up, see (4)— in this case hauling "The Yorkshireman". As is usually the case with Hornby models, the LMS version was made and sold in considerably larger numbers than its companions. Length (engine and tender): 15in (38·1cm).
2 Gauge "0" Hornby No 2 Special, 4-4-0 "County of Bedford" Locomotive, numbered "3821", and Six-Wheeled Tender, Great Western Railway (GWR); 20-volt electric. This locomotive featured in "The Bristolian" express passenger

train set. Length: as (1).
3 Gauge "0", Hornby No 2 Special, 4-4-0 "L1 Class" Locomotive and Six-Wheeled Tender, numbered "1759", Southern Railway (SR); 20-volt electric. Hauling the "Folkestone Flyer" express passenger train set, this was, in terms of sales, certainly the least popular of the series—and is therefore now the scarcest and the most sought after by collectors. Length: as (1).
4 Gauge "0", Hornby No 2 Special, 4-4-0 "Bramham Moor" Locomotive, numbered "201", and Six-Wheeled Tender, London and North Eastern Railway (LNER); 20-volt electric. This model represents an up-date on "Yorkshire", the first of the No 2 Special locomotives, and it featured in the express passenger

train set named "Scarborough Flier". From the mid-1930s, the No 2 Special sets were available in either clockwork or electric. In clockwork, the No 2 Special set consisted of a reversing locomotive with tender; one No 2 Corridor Coach; one No 2 Corridor Composite Coach; twelve A2 Curved Rails, one B1 Straight Rail, and one BBR Straight Brake and Reverse Rail, making up a 5ft 4in x 4ft 6in (1·625m x 1·37m) layout. The E220 Special set in 20-volt electric consisted of an automatic reversing locomotive, with electric headlamp (not present in the examples shown; see introductory note), and tender; two No 2 Corridor Coaches; one No 2 Corridor Composite Coach; and twelve curved and two straight rails, again making up a

layout 5ft 4in x 4ft 6in (1·625m x 1·37m). Sets were priced at £2 12s 0d (£2.60, $3.12) in clockwork, or £3 12s 0d (£3.60, $4.32) in electric. The locomotives and the other set components could, of course, also be purchased as separate items: the electric locomotive, without tender, was priced at £1 17s 6d (£1.87½, $2.25); the clockwork version, without tender, at £1 7s 6d (£1.37½, $1.65); and the tender at 7s 6d (37½p, 45c) for either version. Length: 14·625in (37·15cm).

5 Gauge "0" 4-4-0 "Eton" Locomotive and Six-Wheeled Tender, numbered "900", by Hornby. This representation of a "Schools Class" locomotive of the SR does not belong to the No 2 Special series: it is classified as Series

4, of which it is the only example. Based on No 2 Special components, it is a markedly foreshortened model but is surprisingly convincing in its general proportions and is an interesting example of Hornby's approach to the upper end of its market, with a model nearer-to-prototype and of less "toy-like" quality. Note that it does not have the ugly smokebox headlamp that was fitted on most of the No 2 Special locomotives beneath the "Hornby" label—the latter visible at (1); and note also the effective use of polished brass fittings, an innovation for Hornby at this time. This model was produced only from 1937 until World War II and was available as the E420 20-volt electric model with remote

control (a control lever on the transformer allowed the train to be started, stopped, or reversed, and speed varied to suit the layout), as shown here; or as the No 4C clockwork version. It was priced at £2 2s 6d (£2.12½, ($2.55) in electric, or £1 15s 0d (£1.75, $2.10) in clockwork; the tender being 6s 0d (30p, 36c) extra for either version. Although it had only a comparatively short production run, this locomotive is not particularly rare. However, it is avidly sought after by Hornby collectors, and it will probably prove to be difficult to find a Series 4 locomotive that is in the fine condition of the example shown here. Length (engine and tender): 14·75in (37·465cm).

1-3 Gauge "00" Surburban Southern Electric Set by Triang, Great Britain; comprising R156 Suburban Motor Coach with Powered Bogie Unit (1), and R225 Dummy Suburban Motor Coach, Un-Powered (3); here seen with an additional First Class Coach (2). The two-car Southern Region set was produced in the late 1950s and is an excellent representation, in plastic, of a British commuter train. Triang trains are made by Rovex Models, Margate. The early LMS Pacifics were crude, but quality improved through the 1960s. For a time, items were produced under the Triang-Hornby name: the Hornby name prevailed, and Triang continues to produce excellent Gauge "00" models under the Hornby mark. The set shown is

keenly sought and is not easy to find. Length (each coach): 8·9375in (22·7cm).

4 Gauge "00" Tank Wagon, "Standard" and "Esso" (other side: "Standard" and "Essolub"), tinplate, by Gebrüder Märklin, (West) Germany, dating from either 1939-40 or post-War (it incorporates the automatic coupling introduced in 1939). Many items in Märklin's Gauge "00" series are mirror-images of their Gauge "0" equivalents. Note on this wagon such detail as the brake hut and ladder. Length: 3·75in (9·5cm).

5 Gauge "00" Timber Wagon with Brake Hut, tinplate, by Märklin; again with automatic coupling, dating as (4), and another most attractive continental-style wagon. Length: 3·75in (9·5cm).

6 Gauge "00" Banana Van, "Fyffes", tinplate, by Märklin; a pre-1939 item with claw-type buckeye couplings rather than the automatic couplings seen on (4) and (5). Length: 3·35in (8·5cm).

7 Gauge "00" 2-6-2 Prairie Tank Locomotive, Great Western Railway (GWR), electric, by Graham Farish, Great Britain. This maker appeared in the late 1940s and continued in production into the 1950s. The locomotive shown has a diecast body and metal-rimmed plastic wheels: plastics were used more extensively in other Graham Farish locomotives, which included a Western Region "King Class", Southern Region "West Country" and "Merchant Navy" types, and a Midland Region "Class 5". These models were much inferior to their

Hornby counterparts, although their two-rail electric operation looked vastly better than Hornby's printed-tin track. The wheels were inferior to Hornby castings, permitting no daylight to be seen between the spokes. The locomotives suffered from mechanical defects and, structurally, from warping mazac (zinc alloy). Tender locomotives were motorised in the tender, with a universal coupling to the locomotive gearing. The firm also produced some plastic-bodied Pullman Cars with diecast floors and interiors: these were good models—but the plastic had a tendency to "banana" and the castings were subject to fatigue. Certain Graham Farish items, especially those in Southern Region colours, are now quite

eagerly sought by collectors.
Length: 6·5in (16·51cm).
8 Gauge "00" "Mitropa" Sleeping
Car by Märklin, dating from the
mid-1930s; one of Märklin's earlier
series in this scale, produced
until World War II and, unlike the
nearer-scale vehicles at (11-12),
painted, lined, and transferred.
The attractive little vehicles were
made in many non-German liveries,
including British ones, and are
quite collectable items. Length:
6·9in (17·5cm).
9 Gauge "00" Pullman Coach with
Lights by Trix Twin, Great Britain.
Produced immediately before World
War II and again from the later
1940s, this was one of Trix's
better-looking passenger vehicles
and, like most Trix vehicles, was
lithographed by Winteringham.

Length: 8·75in (22·22cm).
10 Gauge "00" Southern Railway
Passenger Coach by Trix Twin.
Again lithographed by Winteringham,
this example has hook-and-loop
couplings that date it from pre-
1940; the model was reissued
post-War—see (14-15). These short
vehicles were made to complement
Trix's 0-4-0 locomotives; rather
unattractive models, they are
sought only by Trix enthusiasts.
Length: 7in (17·78cm).
11-12 Gauge "00" "Wagons-Lits"
Dining Car (11) and Sleeping Car
(12) by Märklin. These are the
maker's better-length vehicles of
the late 1930s, with a high
standard of detail and convincingly
lithographed in a famous livery.
Many collectors concentrate entirely
on Märklin's Gauge "00" models.

Length: 8·86in (22·5cm).
13 Gauge "00" 4-4-0 Standard LMS
Compound Locomotive, numbered
"1168", and Six-Wheeled Tender,
electric, by Trix Twin. This is a
pre-War specimen of a model that
appeared in the late 1930s and was
reissued after World War II, lasting
into the British Railways period.
Disproportionate in comparison with
its Hornby Dublo equivalents,
this 4-4-0 series included an
LNER "Hunt Class" and an SR
"Schools Class". Trix models are
increasingly collected, but their
appeal is limited. Length (engine
and tender): 8·5in (21·59cm).
14-15 Gauge "00" LMS Passenger
Coaches by Trix Twin; post-War
examples of the short coach at (10),
seen here in different livery.
Length: 7in (17·78cm).

16-20 Gauge "00" "Table Top" 2-4-0
Tank Locomotive (16) by Gebrüder
Bing, Germany; shown with a train
of which (17) may not be by Bing;
(18) and (19) are Bing GWR coaches;
and (20) is a Bing LNER coach. All
these items are a little shabby
but could be restored; this would
be well worthwhile, as Bing "Table
Top Railways", dating from the
mid-1920s to the early 1930s, are
now quite collectable. The
locomotives were made in
clockwork, as shown, or electric.
Lengths (locomotive): 3·75in
(9·5cm); (coach): 3·25in (8·25cm).
21 Gauge "00" Caboose by Trix Twin,
Great Britain, c1953. This is a
more than usually interesting Trix
item, since it depicts one of the
caboose cars so popular with US
collectors. Length: 4·5in (11·43cm).

1 Gauge "0" Four-Wheeled Tank Locomotive, Model "300" and numbered thus, made by Bowman, Norwich, Great Britain. All sizes of the Gauge "0" steam trains made by Bowman from the 1920s until production ended in the late 1930s are shown on this spread. In London and North Eastern Railway (LNER) livery—it was also available in London, Midland & Scottish (LMS) colours—this locomotive is fitted with oscillating cylinders, a safety-valve, and a water-level cock on the firebox. It is shown in its original wooden box—which bears the pencilled price "21/-" (£1 1s 0d, £1.05, $1.26)—with its instruction leaflet. Length: 8·5in (21·59cm). As is apparent from this and the other Bowman

items shown, these locomotives, although excellent runners, tend to be of clumsy appearance and generally over-scale. The firm was originally known for its stationary steam engines made to drive Meccano models, and also produced a popular series of wooden-hulled steamboats.

2 Gauge "0" 4-4-2 Locomotive and Six-Wheeled Tender, numbered "4472", by Bowman; supposedly a representation of the "Flying Scotsman", in LNER livery and bearing that famous locomotive's number—but there the resemblance ends! A massive and unwieldy spirit-fired steam model, it is nevertheless a splendid performer: it was introduced in 1927 at the British Industries Fair, London, where, according

to Bowman's publicitiy, it ran continuously for 187 *real* miles (300km) hauling six tinplate coaches. The copper steam-pipe leading to the cylinders, and the typical Bowman safety-valve, used on all the maker's models, are seen to advantage in the photograph. For some reason, possibly to make them appear to be cheaper, engine and tender were sold in separate boxes, priced at £1 7s 6d (£1.37½, $1.65) and 7s 6d (37½p, 45c) respectively. Length (engine and tender): 19·25in (48·89cm).

3 Gauge "0" 0-6-0 Tank Locomotive (a type popularly known as a "Jinty"), numbered "489" and in Great Western Railway (GWR) livery, by Archangel Models, Great Britain. This model of a

locomotive of c1900 dates from the mid-1970s and its maker is still in production. The well-proportioned locomotive is fitted with a twin-burner spirit lamp, has an inside cylinder with displacement lubrication, and features slip-eccentric reversing. Note the large throttle handle at the rear of the cab. Its small, turned cast-iron wheels—the central pair unflanged to enable it to negotiate sharp curves—give it excellent pulling power: it will run for 15-20 minutes with a train of up to six bogie coaches or 12 goods wagons. Length: 9·5in (24·13cm).

4 Gauge "0" 4-4-0 Locomotive and Six-Wheeled Tender, numbered "6285", made by Winteringham, Bassett-Lowke's Northampton-

based subsidiary. This model, made in steam only, was called "Enterprise" by Bassett-Lowke and first appeared in the late 1920s: it was later available in kit form, as well as ready-made, and remained in the Catalogue until the 1960s. It is equipped with displacement lubrication; ie, water pressure in the boiler is utilized, via a tube, to force oil into the cylinders. It has piston-valve cylinders and is, in the opinion of the author, who has run this example regularly for some 20 years, the most efficient Gauge "0" locomotive ever made commercially in respect of power and long-running: it will haul six tinplate bogie coaches for 45 minutes on a single filling. Length (engine and

tender): 18in (45·72cm). Note the the number of the tender refers not to a real locomotive but, in fact, to the telephone number at the time of production of Bassett-Lowke's shop in High Holborn, London!

5 Gauge "0" Four-Wheeled Locomotive in LNER livery by Bowman, the smallest of the firm's range, only 7in (17·78cm) long. With a single oscillating cylinder in the cab, it is in spite of its diminutive size a fairly efficient runner, travelling for 10-12 minutes on a single filling. It was sold in a wooden box (like all Bowman models), complete with filling funnel, lubricating oil, and instruction leaflet, at a price of 10s 6d (52½p, 63c) in the late 1920s-1930s.

6 Gauge "0" 0-4-0 Locomotive and Six-Wheeled Tender by Bassett-Lowke: a model with a pronounced Carette appearance and, in fact, made for Bassett-Lowke in Northampton in the 1920s from pressings acquired from Germany after the French-owned, Nuremburg-based firm of Carette went out of business during World War I. Produced also in Gauge "1", and in steam only, it was available in the liveries of the Midland Railway, as shown, GWR, L&NWR, and Caledonian Railway (blue). It has a vaporising spirit lamp, piston-valve cylinders, displacement lubrication, and unusually for Bassett-Lowke at this time, slip-eccentric reversing. Length (engine

and tender): 13in (33·02cm).

7 Gauge "0" 0-4-0 Tank Locomotive, numbered "265" and in LNER livery, by Bowman. The over-scale character of Bowman's models is particularly evident here: with a length of 11in (27·94cm) and a maximum height of nearly 5in (12·7cm), this model is virtually in 9mm scale, rather than the 7mm scale normal for Gauge "0". Aesthetically, Bowman's locomotives have little to offer, but they were nevertheless very popular with collectors in the 1970s, when prices rocketed. They are presently out of fashion (although, in the author's opinion, only temporarily) and the would-be collector should hesitate before paying excessive sums for these items.

1 Gauge "0" Brake Corridor Coach, Great Western Railway (GWR), made by Winteringham for Bassett-Lowke, Great Britain, and catalogued at 12s 6d (62½p, 75c) in 1938. With the demise of its German supplier, Gebrüder Bing, in the earlier 1930s, Bassett-Lowke had to turn elsewhere for lithographed tinplate construction—and this is one of many items made for Bassett-Lowke in the 1930s by the Northampton-based firm of Winteringham. This is one of a fine series of coaches that appeared in the four major liveries, the mainline GWR version shown being the most convincing, and the Southern Railway (SR) the least successful. Winteringham ,it may be noted, chose a longer and better length that that of Bing's 1921 series. These vehicles are

quite collectable, especially the GWR and SR versions. Length: 13in (33·02cm).

2 Gauge "0" Travelling Post Office Vehicle, London, Midland & Scottish Railway (LMS), by Winteringham for Bassett-Lowke and catalogued at £1 1s 0d (£1.05, $1.26) in 1938. Another finely-lithographed corridor mainline vehicle which, like (1), replaced a rather shorter predecessor. Like the earlier model, it features an ingenious method—using a trip-mechanism and ramp-rail and net unit—for picking up or dropping mail while the train is moving. This is one of the most collectable of all the Winteringham bogie vehicles. Length: 13in (33·02cm).

3 Gauge "0" 20-Ton Goods Brake Van, GWR, by Winteringham for

Bassett-Lowke; see also (12). The appearance of these lithographed vehicles was a little inconsistent in terms of realism: Winteringham's brake and goods vans seem a little over-scale in height. Nevertheless, they are interesting to collect, since the series is small enough for a complete run to be found. Length: 5·75in (14·605cm).

4 Gauge "0" Tank Wagon, "Pratt's Spirit", by Winteringham for Bassett-Lowke, 1930s. This is a most convincing model and is one of the most pleasing Bassett-Lowke wagons. It is also about the rarest of the series and is therefore highly prized by collectors. Length: 5·75in (14·605cm).

5 Gauge "0" Open Wagon, SR, by Winteringham for Bassett-Lowke, 1930s. In this series, all four

major liveries were catered for by at least one open wagon and one covered van. The SR version shown is probably the hardest to find, but these vehicles were made in considerable numbers and are all fairly common. Note that an austere series of open wagons, covered vans, and brake vehicles was made after World War II: these are so drab that it seems that no collector really desires them! Length: 5in (12·7cm).

6 Gauge "0" Standard LNER Flatrol Wagon with Cable Drum, Winteringham for Bassett-Lowke, 1930s; see also (13). With its huge "Callender" drum, this is quite a convincing model of its LNER prototype: a well wagon was also available without load. Like the tank wagons, these vehicles are highly

desirable. Expensive for a tinplate goods vehicle of the time—priced 8s 0d (40p, 48c) in 1938—they were not made in great numbers and are therefore quite rare. Length: 12in (30·48cm).

7 Gauge "0" Private Owner's 12-Ton Open Wagon, Winteringham for Bassett-Lowke, 1930s. Bassett-Lowke's private owner vehicles, illustrating the maker's habit of self-advertising, are in themselves a collectable range. Open wagons bearing Bassett-Lowke's name were available well before World War I, and some of these, made by Carette in Gauges "0", "1", and "2", are avidly sought after. This item in attractive dark-lead-grey and yellow livery, is also highly desirable and is not easy to find. Length: 5·75in (14·605cm).

8 Gauge "0" Oil Tank Wagon, "Esso" —see also (11)—by Winteringham for Bassett-Lowke, 1930s. These most attractive tank wagons are highly collectable and are not at all easy to find. Length: 5·75in (14·605cm).

9 Gauge "0" 0-6-0 Goods Locomotive, numbered "4256", and Six-Wheeled Tender, in LMS goods colours (also available for LNER), Winteringham for Bassett-Lowke, 1930s. This small locomotive in lithographed tinplate was available in both electric, as shown, and clockwork versions. It was made in quantity throughout the 1930s and appeared again after World War II, ending in a rather drab, unlined, matt black British Railways (BR) form. A freelance model (ie, one based on no particular prototype), it

displays the somewhat unimaginative approach to freight locomotives manifested by many makers of toy trains. This is an easy model to find in any style. Length (engine and tender): 14·5in (36·83cm).

10 Gauge "0" Milk Tank Wagon, "United Dairies", lettered for GWR, by Winteringham for Bassett-Lowke, 1930s. This is perhaps the most exotic of the Winteringham goods vehicles, finely-detailed and extremely well-proportioned; it is very collectable and will be quite hard to find. It is interesting to compare its price with its Hornby counterpart—see (3), *pages 84-85:* the Hornby wagon cost 4s 6d (22½p, 27c) in 1938; the Winteringham/Bassett-Lowke version cost 5s 6d (27½p, 33c). Length: 5·75in (14·605cm).

11 Gauge "0" Oil Tank Wagon, "Mobiloil"; as (8). Perhaps because of its darker colouring, it is less attractive than the "Esso" version, but still most collectable. Length: 5·75in (14·605cm).

12 Gauge "0" 20-Ton Goods Brake Van, LMS; as (3), but somehow more convincing in terms of artwork than its GWR counterpart. The LMS version is the easiest to find. Length: 5·75in (14·605cm).

13 Gauge "0" Standard LNER Flatrol Wagon with Boiler Load; as (6), with different load. This is the most attractive of the bogie goods vehicles in the series, and has another example of Bassett-Lowke's self-advertising on the side of the boiler. A very collectable item, it is now fairly hard to find. Length: 12in (30·48cm).

1 Gauge "0" 2-6-2 Suburban Tank Locomotive, Great Western Railway (GWR), numbered "6105"; available from Bassett-Lowke from the late 1930s until World War II. This model, almost entirely handmade and well-proportioned although plain, was made in 8-10 volt DC, 20-volt AC, and clockwork, and incorporates such distinctive features as a brass safety-valve casing and a copper chimney-top. In these models, sheet-steel was soft-soldered with the use of an acid flux, and it may be found that, because of insufficient cleaning at the time of manufacture, "bubbling" has occurred on the paintwork in areas of complex detail. Although this sign of rusting can look unpleasant,

especially on the underside or interior, there is no need to fear further corrosion provided the model is kept in a dry place. If the condition is very bad, however, it is advisable to take steps to neutralize or cover it. This is quite a rare model. Length: 11·375in (28·89cm).
2 Gauge "0" 4-6-0 "Royal Scot" Locomotive, numbered "6100", and Six-Wheeled Tender, London, Midland & Scottish Railway (LMS). This 12-volt electric model dating from c1937 is the final version of Bassett-Lowke's standard tinplate lithographed model, now slightly improved, hand-painted, fitted with smoke deflectors, and with a new Stanier-type high-sided tender. Both lithographed and hand-painted versions are

not too hard to find; the former seem to manifest a considerable range of LMS reds, from a rather garish bright shade to a near-correct crimson. Available in electric or clockwork, it reappeared after World War II in clockwork only and in a black, red-lined LMS livery. Later, Bassett-Lowke totally altered the model, introducing a taper-boiler and firebox and a new front end. Length (engine and tender): 18·375in (46·67cm).
3 Gauge "0" 4-4-0 LMS Standard Compound Locomotive, numbered "1063", and Six-Wheeled Tender. This model was available from the early 1930s in clockwork or electric: the one shown is an electric version, entirely lithographed, dating from c1949.

This Bassett-Lowke model was a good representation of its prototype, but post-War versions are generally of a much better colour than pre-War examples. However, a run of post-War lithographed models (not including the example shown) appeared in a totally spurious brown livery. Bassett-Lowke Compounds are by no means rare. Length (engine and tender): 15·75in (40·005cm).
4 Gauge "0" 2-6-4 LMS Standard Tank Locomotive, numbered "2603". This Bassett-Lowke model was available in electric or clockwork from the late 1903s, succeeding a rarer Märklin-bodied counterpart —see note at (6). The example shown is an electric version dating from c1949: it is

Right: *The close-up front view of the Märklin-bodied Bassett-Lowke 5XP-Type "Newfoundland" locomotive at (6) shows how the polished smokebox hinges contribute to the effect of this excellent model. Note that the buffer-beam on the Märklin-bodied locomotive does not feature Bassett-Lowke's usual ugly coupling and slot.*

interesting to note that the price rose from around £9 0s 0d (£9.00, $10.80) pre-War to £23 6s 0d (£23.30, $27.96) in 1949, and to more than £60 0s 0d (£60.00, $72.00) in the 1960s. Length: 12·75in (32·385cm).

5 Gauge "0" 4-6-0 "Arsenal" Locomotive, numbered "2848", and Six-Wheeled Tender, London and North Eastern Railway (LNER), available in electric, as shown, or clockwork, from the mid-1930s until World War II. This most convincing model by Bassett-Lowke of a "Sandringham"-type locomotive of the Eastern Region of the LNER is one of the "Football" series: another of the models was named "Huddersfield Town", and the non-football choice "Melton Hall" also appeared.

Probably not many were made—and surviving examples tend to be in truly terrible condition. The example shown has been restored professionally by its present owner from a poor state. With shabby or poorly-repainted models, there is little alternative other than to strip and repaint, although it is sometimes possible to retrieve and restore the original paintwork. Collectors differ on this subject: some advocate no restoration, but this seems unacceptable in the case of badly chipped paintwork, lettering rubbed away, visible areas of rust, soldered seams split, dents, or badly enamel-painted patches. How does restoration affect value? For an unrestored model, we may say that

if the mint original is worth 100 per cent, a slightly used example may be worth 70 per cent; a shabby one, 50 per cent or less; and a really bad example around 25 per cent. A professionally-restored model, capturing fully the style and finish of the maker's original, should fall into, or even above, the 70 per cent bracket. This is a rule-of-thumb: there will be many exceptions in the areas both of steam and of very rare models. The locomotive shown here is avidly sought by collectors. Length (engine and tender): 17·25in (43·815cm).

6 Gauge "0" 4-6-0 "Newfoundland" 5XP-Type Locomotive, numbered "5573", and Six-Wheeled Tender, LMS, electric. Around the mid-

1930s, Bassett-Lowke engaged Märklin to produce the upper bodywork for certain runs of its more expensive models: a GWR "King", an SR "Schools", an LMS Tank Locomotive—see note at (4), and the 5XP-Type seen here. Most 5XPs were not named, but "Newfoundland" was added in accordance with LMS practice, and a black "Silver Jubilee" also appeared. All the Märklin-bodied models are very highly valued and rare, and the example shown is likely to be one of the more difficult to acquire. Bassett-Lowke's British-made versions of a later period, named "Conqueror" and then "Victory", are likely to be easier to find. Length (engine and tender): 18·25in (46·355cm).

1 Gauge "0" Bogie Suburban Coach, in London, Midland & Scottish Railway colours, by Leeds Model Company (LMC), Great Britain, dating from the mid- to late-1930s. LMC sought to produce Gauge "0" items to a high standard, and the company's products are models rather than toys. The example shown demonstrates a rather strange attempt at an inexpensive coach: the body and roof are of good-quality cardboard, the ends are diecast, and the base is wood. The firms' usual fragile cast bogies are fitted. Most LMC coaches were wood-bodied, with metal roofs, and with printed paper artwork stuck to the sides and ends. Although interesting and unusual, this vehicle is not really an

important collector's item. Length: 13in (33·02cm).

2 Gauge "0" Pullman Supply Car, "Brenda", by Bond's ("Bond's o' Euston Road"), London. Probably dating from the 1950s, this is from some very small batches made by Bond's to depict Southern Railway (SR) electric Pullmans: this example was found as part of a very handsome five-car motorized "Brighton Belle" set. The style and shape of the vehicles was excellent, but all were painted a drab tan-brown: the present owner (a professional restorer) has repainted, as seen, in Pullman livery. Such models are eagerly sought by model railway operators. Length: 16·75in (42·5cm).

3 Gauge "0" Pullman Car,

"Grosvenor", by Milbro (Mills Brothers of Sheffield), 1930s. Up to World War II, Milbro made a magnificent selection of Gauge "0" rolling stock. The example shown was purchased in a shabby state: the owner has redecorated the lower umber panel in Pullman style and has added such embellishments as roof fan covers, destination-board brackets and boards, brass hand-rails, and interior detail. Like (2), this vehicle would be of more interest to a general collector and operator than to a tinplate purist. Length: 18·5in (49·99cm).

4 Gauge "0" Six-Wheeled Guard's Van of the SR (South Eastern & Chatham Railway), thought to be by the Windsor Model Company of Great Britain, and probably

dating from the mid-1930s. It was acquired with a rake of similar Southern passenger bogie vehicles—most attractive cars, well made of wood with some card application, and with imaginative painted detail and fittings. This would be irresistible to SR specialists, although not highly collectable in the usual sense. Length: 9in (22·86cm).

5 Gauge "0" 0-6-0 Goods Locomotive, numbered "17651", and Six-Wheeled Tender, electric, by Leeds Model Company, late 1930s. This is a well-proportioned model of an ex-Caledonian Railway freight locomotive, seen here in post-1923 LMS livery. It is one of the simpler of LMC's handsome locomotives: the range included an LNER "Sir Sam Fay"

Class and 4-4-0 "Director", a fine "Claughton", and, most commonly seen, a series of small tank locomotives—see (8)—in LMS, LNER, and SR colours. In spite of their high quality, LMC models seem to rank low on the collector's list. Length (engine and tender): 15in (38cm).

6 Gauge "0" Private Owner Open Wagon, by R.F. Stedman & Co., Ltd. (later to become Leeds Model Company), early 1930s. This is one of a large series, marketed either ready-made or in kit form, of wooden wagons with lithographed paper stickers, link couplings, and cast axle guards, buffers and wheels. There were several private owner's names in the series: this one bears the name of the parent factory. Again, not

of great interest to the non-specialist collector. Length: 5·625in (14·29cm).

7 Gauge "0" Tank Wagon, "BP Motor Spirit", by Leeds Model Company, mid-to-late 1930s. These are delightful models, with transferred and painted tinplate tanks, diecast detail, and wood chassis. LMC later was probably the first maker to produce both wagons and passenger coaches in bakelite. Length: 6·25in (15·9cm).

8 Gauge "0" 0-6-0 LNER Tank Locomotive, numbered "8304", in 12-volt electric, by Leeds Model Company, c1950. Attractive but non-scale, these models were made both before and after World War II. Most examples had a mazac (zinc alloy) chassis: this was subject to fatigue, and

models will be found, presentable above the footplate, but with the remaining parts looking like crazy-paving, or of "banana" shape! However, a competent model engineer should be able to devise a new chassis which will improve the model's performance without affecting its collectability—which is, in any case, limited in appeal, since these locomotives represent the more commercial aspect of LMC. Length: 8·25in (20·95cm).

9 Gauge "0" Travelling Post Office, in LMS livery, by Exley, Great Britain, dating from around 1936. This is one of a large range of coaches made by the Bradford-based firm. Pre-War examples display a rather more casual approach to finish than

their post-War counterparts, perhaps because, pre-War, all lettering was painted on (as will be obvious from a close study of the lettering "Royal Mail" on the example shown here). However, the vehicles have considerable charm and look well when running behind large locomotives. These Exley vehicles have aluminium bodies, with cast ends and wooden floors. Like the other rather specialised models by the comparatively lesser-known British makers shown on this spread, they mostly have only limited appeal for collectors whose main interest lies in displaying their models; however, they are eagerly sought after by those who run Gauge "0" railways. Length: 16·5in (41·91cm).

All the trains shown on this spread were photographed at the London Toy and Model Museum, October House, 21/23 Craven Hill, London W2.

1-3 Cast-Iron Floor Train by a American toymaker, dating from around 1880. This is, of course, very much an "odd one out" on this spread, but it is interesting to study this early item in contrast to the much later trains by American makers also shown here. It is possible that this train was made by the Kenton Hardware Company, Kenton, Ohio, a noted maker of cast-iron toys, but precise identification of these unpowered, pull/push-along toys in a material so favoured by American toymakers is difficult, since they were extremely

popular during the later 19th century and were produced by many makers throughout the United States, few of them bearing any manufacturer's mark. The train shown here, made in a scale slightly smaller than Gauge "1", is headed by a 4-4-0 Baldwin "Wild West"-type Locomotive (3), with a Four-Wheeled Tender, hauling two eight-wheeled cars: a Parlour Car (2) and a Combine (Brake End) (3), both of which are attractively embossed "Chicago, Rock Island and Pacific Railroad Co". This is a rare item. Lengths (locomotive and tender): 14in (35·56cm); (each car): 12in (30·48cm).
4-6 Gauge "0" "English Flyer" Clockwork Train Set, made for the British market by American Flyer, USA, and dating from around

1925. This is an unusual and somewhat rare item, since it apparently represents an isolated attempt by American Flyer to break into the British market then dominated by Bing/Bassett-Lowke and Hornby. The small four-wheeled Locomotive (6) is made of cast-iron; the four-wheeled Tender numbered "No.120", the Passenger Coach (5), and the Mail Van (4), are all in lithographed tinplate. All the items are in the livery of the Great Northern Railway (GNR), and the legend "English Flyer" appears on the carriage ends and on the buffer beam of the locomotive. Note, however, that no buffers are fitted to any of the items in the set. This simple clockwork train, which was marketed as a boxed set complete with a circle of tinplate track,

resembles the category of cheaper toy trains that were produced at this time by British and other makers in competition with Hornby. These are generally of less appeal to the collector than Hornby items—although this particular set, as noted above, is both interesting and unusual and would be well worth having. Cheaper sets in this category were produced in Great Britain by Chad Valley, Mettoy and other makers. Length (train overall): 21in (53·34cm).
7-10 Gauge "00" Electric Train Set by the Lionel Corporation, New York, USA. This item illustrates a most interesting, and short-lived, development: Lionel's venture into Gauge "00". Lionel trains in this gauge—built to "00" scale but running on track of 19mm (0·75in)

gauge—appeared in the late 1930s and early 1940s but, unfortunately, did not reappear after World War II, although Lionel then became busy on the Gauge "H0" scene, working in that field in conjunction with Rivarossi from 1959 (the year in which Lionel became part of the Roy M. Cohn Group, continuing production thereafter as The Lionel Toy Corporation). The attractive and well-detailed diecast train shown here is headed by a 4-6-4 Hudson Locomotive, numbered "5432", and Twelve-Wheeled Tender (10), finished for the New York Central Railroad. This model was inspired by Lionel's famous, earlier fine-scale Hudson locomotive in Gauge "0". It was made in Gauge "00", to a scale of 4mm, in 1938, when it was fitted for three-rail

electric traction (as in the example shown). From 1939 until 1942, when production ceased following the entry of the United States into World War II, it was issued with a two-rail pickup. The train it is here shown hauling consists of a High-Sided Gondola (9) of the Southern Pacific Lines; a Box Car (8), "Lionel Lines"; and a Caboose (7), of the Pennsylvania Railroad. The Hudson, the premier locomotive used on the New York-Chicago run, occupies about the same place in the affections of American railway buffs as, say, the "Flying Scotsman" does in those of British railway enthusiasts. Many manufacturers produced models of this locomotive, the largest probably being the "2½in" Gauge non-motorised version by Gilbert,

USA. In the smaller scales, probably the most sought-after and valuable Hudson is that made in Gauge "0" by Märklin, Germany, in the late 1930s, although Märklin's version has few pretensions towards scale. In Gauge "H0", models were produced by Graham Farish, Great Britain, probably in an attempt to break into the American market, and by Rivarossi, Italy, the latter being a very fine streamlined model. Length (train overall): 33in (83·82cm).

11-12 Gauge "0" Twin-Unit Diesel Locomotive of the Western Pacific Railroad, by Lionel, maker's catalogue number 2355A, dating from 1953. It is modelled on an "F3 Type" Diesel locomotive and is fitted with "Magnatraction", a magnetic device patented by Lionel that was

designed to provide for greater rail adhesion, and thus give increased hauling capability. Although it is a fairly late item, fitted for three-rail electric operation, this Lionel model, constructed mainly of diecast alloy, is nicely detailed and well finished. Length (overall): 26in (66·04cm).

13-16 Gauge "0" "Lionel Lines" "Streamliner" (thus catalogued by the maker, and numbered "1700"; but sometimes known as the "Burlington Zephyr"), made by Lionel in 1935-37. Lionel's version of the streamline diesel train as a four-car articulated unit is in aluminized tinplate finish. It is fitted for three-rail electric operation. Such sets are quite hard to find outside the USA. Length (train overall): 40in (101·6cm).

All the trains shown on this spread were photographed at the London Toy and Model Museum, October House, 21/23 Craven Hill, London W2.

1 and **7** "Standard Gauge" Electric Locomotive (1), maker's number 402E, and Combine Pullman Car (7), by Lionel, USA, dating from around 1920. A familiar item to all collectors of American trains, this massive locomotive in the maker's Standard Gauge, of 2·125in (54mm) measured between the rails, is made of tinplate. It is on twin trucks (bogies), one of which is powered for a three-rail pickup. Although it is not apparent in the example shown here, this model is usually to be found lettered "N.Y.C.

Lines" (New York Central), although neither the locomotive nor the Pullman car is in that railway's colours. The strangely unorthodox livery is believed to have resulted from Lionel's employment of an Italian designer who apparently knew a great deal about Italian railways but little of American lines! Nevertheless, both locomotive and Pullman car are by no means unattractive items and they are eagerly sought after by American collectors in particular. In Great Britain, too, interest in Lionel's models is increasing and there are now, to the author's knowledge, several British enthusiasts who collect and run Lionel trains. Lengths (locomotive): 16·5in (41·91cm); (Pullman car): 18in (45·72cm).

2-3 "Standard Gauge" Four-Wheeled Electric Locomotive (3) and Twin-Truck Pullman Car (2), "Pleasant View", numbered "790", by Dorfan, USA, dating from 1926. The locomotive is of diecast zinc alloy; the Pullman car is tinplate. The Dorfan company was founded in Newark, New Jersey, in the early 1920s by the Forchheimer Brothers, formerly of the Kraus Toy Factory, Nuremburg, Germany. The Forchheimers brought with them to the United States John Koerber, formerly a craftsman with Gebrüder Bing. Dorfan initially made electric trains in Gauge "0", and from 1926 in Standard Gauge, the latter items by Dorfan's newly-developed process of pressure diecasting in zinc alloy. The method of construc-

tion of this toy is, therefore, of interest. The locomotive body was cast in two halves, each shell containing all the necessary axle bearings, lugs and fittings to accommodate the electric motor and wheel assembly. This was simply inserted into one half, which was then firmly pressed into conjunction with the other half, making a tight fit that required no nuts or bolts to secure it. An interesting refinement in Dorfan locomotives was the use of ball bearings on the motor drive and as axle bearings. Dorfan was a victim of the Depression, and although production continued into the 1930s it then consisted only of cheap toy trains in Gauge "0", none of the attractive Standard Gauge items reappearing.

The underside of the Pullman car seen here bears the label: "Dorfan Co, Newark, New Jersey"; it is, however, possible that this pleasing vehicle may have been made for Dorfan by Kraus in Nuremburg. Lengths (locomotive): 12in (30·48cm); (Pullman car): 13·5in (34·29cm).

4 Gauge "0" Buffet Car, numbered "No.130", 'The Ives Railway Lines'; this car forms part of the Ives train shown at (5-6). It may be noted here that Ives was an early entrant into the Gauge "0" scene in the United States and was very successful in the earlier years of this gauge. However, when Lionel concentrated its efforts on Standard Gauge, Ives chose to put emphasis on Gauge "1". The company only entered the Standard

Gauge market at a later date, around 1921, when it was more or less forced to do so by the market pressure exerted by Lionel, American Flyer, and Dorfan. The Ives company suffered badly during the market slump of 1929 and these problems resulted in its takeover by its major competitors, Lionel, Hafner, and American Flyer. Lionel alone continued to produce Ives models—as Lionel-Ives, at Irvington, New Jersey—in 1931-32, but in the latter year the famous name of Ives vanished from the market. Length: 9in (22·86cm).

5-6 Gauge "0" Four-Wheeled Electric Locomotive (6), numbered "3258", and Parlour Car (5), "Saratoga", numbered "No.129"; with the Buffet Car shown at (4), these items make up an electric

train set made by Ives, Bridgeport, Conn., USA, and dating from around 1912. The locomotive, lettered "The Ives Railway Lines" and "NYC & HR" (New York Central & Hudson Railroad), is constructed chiefly of cast-iron and, despite its four-wheel arrangement, is not unlike its prototype. The parlour car and buffet car are both in printed tinplate. It is interesting to note that this locomotive was available also in clockwork, a feature unique to Ives among American makers of toy trains at that time. Lengths (locomotive): 8·5in (21·59cm); (each car): 9in (22·86cm).

7 "Standard Gauge" Combine Pullman Car by Lionel; see note at (1), above, for details.

8 Floor Toy Train, probably dating from the mid-1950s and by

a maker of unknown nationality identified only as "Zak". Something of a mystery item, this appears at first glance to be an attractive and well-proportioned Gauge "0" train. It is, indeed an attractive and well-made toy of pleasing proportions—but it is actually a friction-powered floor toy, made of tinplate and with rubber wheels. It represents the Union Pacific Railroad's famous "Flying Yankee" as a twin articulated unit and is lettered "Union Pacific" and "New York-S.Francisco". The ends of the units bear the maker's mark "Zak", which will probably mean as little to other collectors of railway toys as it does to the present author. It is, possibly, a Japanese-made item. Length (overall): 23in (58·42cm).

1 Gauge "0" Caboose, Maker's Catalogue Number 657 (all Lionel items display a serial number, visible on the side of this vehicle), by The Lionel Corporation, New York, USA, dating from the 1930s. Note also the "Lionel Lines" plaque on this eight-wheeled (two bogies) caboose. Throughout the 1930s and early 1940s, and again after World War II, Lionel produced a wide range of very robustly built rolling stock in pressed steel, both in Gauge "0" and in the much larger "Standard Gauge". Although perhaps not as attractive in appearance as some of their European-made contemporaries, these are well-made vehicles, incorporating brass trimmings and such detail as brake handles, axle boxes, end ladders,

pressed rivets, and the like. It is interesting to note that exported items sold at comparatively high prices in Great Britain: the caboose shown here was priced at 10s 0d (50p, 60c) in the late 1930s. Most of these vehicles, including the later, better-proportioned, plastic-bodied examples, are sought by Lionel collectors, particularly in the USA. Length: 6·75in (17·145cm).

2 Gauge "0" Flat Car (Lumber Wagon), Catalogue No 651, by Lionel, 1930s. The eight-wheeled (two bogies) wagon is loaded with lumber that may be removed and replaced with other freight. Lumber wagons of this type, and shorter four-wheeled versions, were boxed in some of Lionel's smaller freight train sets. These wagons are very easy

for the collector to find, even outside the USA. The wagon shown was priced at 9s 6d (47½p, 57c) in Britain in 1940; a major British retailer was Gamage's, London, and many veteran British collectors will remember with affection that store's famous operating Lionel railway. Length: 6·75in (17·145cm).

3 Gauge "0" 2-4-2 Locomotive and Twelve-Wheeled Oil Tender, Catalogue No 255E, by Lionel. Produced throughout the 1930s, and electric-powered like all Lionel locomotives, this is one of the maker's de luxe models: extremely strongly built, comparatively well proportioned, and of truly impressive appearance. It is fitted with an operating headlamp and illuminated firebox, and, on the example shown, a whistle mechanism in the tender

(although according to Lionel's Catalogue, model 255E had no whistle; No 255W being thus equipped). These models incorporated a large amount of mazac (zinc alloy): this material in its pre-War form was liable to fatigue, and some of these fine locomotives will now be found with areas warped, cracked, or missing. However, many replacement parts are available in the USA, and these splendid machines are eagerly collected items. Length (engine and tender): 19in (48·26cm).

4 Gauge "0" Remote Control Streamline Outfit (less one unit; see below), Catalogue No 751E, by Lionel, 1930s. Based on the famous "City of Portland" of the Union Pacific Railroad, this finely-made pressed steel and diecast set

is perhaps one of Lionel's most convincing models, faithfully reproducing the detail of the prototype. It incorporates illuminated cars, coloured tail warning lights, and a remote-controlled whistle mechanism. Ingenious snap-fix articulated joints make the units easily detachable—and the tail car has been omitted from this photograph for reasons of space. The remote-controlled 20-volt front unit is only just powerful enough to pull the heavy train from rest—but once it is really rolling, its performance is truly impressive. A silver-coloured version was also produced. The whole of the front end, rear end, and floors of the train are largely of mazac construction and are subject to

fatigue, but in good structural condition these sets are highly desirable and are quite rare, especially outside the USA. Length (as shown): 46in (116·84cm).
5 Gauge "0" Super Detail Scale Model "Hudson", numbered "5344", and Twelve-Wheeled Tender, Catalogue No 700E, by Lionel, 1930s. This is one of the most important items for the Lionel collector: a truly magnificent model of a 4-6-4 locomotive of the New York Central Railroad, the engine is fitted with a working headlamp, illuminated firebox, and operating tender whistle. The 15-volt AC motor and the gearing are of exceptionally high quality, giving a marvellous performance. Lionel used an all-diecast set of components on this model, so the first consideration

for any collector is to check the condition of all cast parts. Fatigue, and missing pieces, are all too common; but spares are available. The example shown, although an excellent one, displays signs of fatigue on the smokebox door, as well as lacking the boiler-mounted hooter and the coal deck on the tender. Beautifully-made cars were issued to run with this locomotive, thus making up the Lionel "Rail Chief", and it was also later produced in a slightly cheaper version. A Gauge "00" version was also made: the only locomotive in that gauge made by Lionel in the 1930s. Number 700E "Hudsons" are very rare and consequently are extremely valuable items. Length (engine and tender): 23·5in (59·69cm).

6 Gauge "0" Illuminated Observation Car, Catalogue No 614, by Lionel, dating from around 1940. Like the maker's freight rolling stock—see (1)—Lionel passenger cars, usually finished in red or blue, were made of pressed steel and appeared in both Gauge "0" and the larger "Standard Gauge". The range included Pullman Cars and Baggage Vans. Lionel passenger vehicles of the type shown here are distinctly under-length, although they present an acceptable appearance when running with the shorter electric- or steam-outline locomotives. None of the shorter-length vehicles is scarce, but some of the larger, de luxe passenger vehicles are highly-prized collector's items. Length: 10·5in (26·67cm).

All the trains and accessories shown on this spread were photographed at the London Toy and Model Museum, October House, 21/23 Craven Hill, London W2.

Toy train collectors of a purist turn of mind may be moved to protest that two of the items shown on this spread—the "Easter Bunny Express" by Marx (5), and the "Donald Duck Hand Car" by Lionel (6)—are not trains at all, but rather mechanical novelty toys. To which objection, the author makes reply that both these items were supplied with tinplate track and were fitted with flanged wheels to run on it: they are trains—of a sort!—and it would be a pity if a book devoted to all kinds of toy trains could not find room for

such attractive and amusing (and very collectable) oddities. Nevertheless, it must be admitted that their appeal is likely to be to the collector of tinplate toys in general, rather than to the dedicated railway enthusiast.

1 Standard Gauge "Lionel Corporation" Power House, made by The Lionel Corporation, New York, USA, and believed to date from around 1926. This nicely-proportioned tinplate building is intended realistically to accommodate the transformer used to supply electric power to a Lionel Standard Gauge railway layout. It is interesting to compare this item with the similar approach adopted by Jep, France; see (1),

pages 122-123. This is obviously a most desirable item for any collector who wishes to run Lionel trains. Dimensions of base: 10in x 9in (25·4cm x 22·86cm).

2 Standard Gauge "Lionel Flagman", made by Lionel at around the same time as the "Power House" at (1), in the mid-1920s. The tinplate warning sign is lettered "Railroad Crossing/Look Out for the Locomotive", and the arm of the tinplate flagman is articulated. Maximum height of sign: 7in (17·78cm).

3 "Railway Crossing" Post, made by American Flyer, USA (lettered on its cross-arm "American Flyer R.R."), and dating from around 1920. This tinplate accessory is suitable for use with Standard Gauge layouts. Height: 6·75in (17·145cm).

4 Standard Gauge "Railway Crossing" Post, by Lionel, dating from the mid-1920s. This tinplate accessory, rather more elaborate than the American Flyer version at (3), is electrically wired to display a green or a red light, and bears the legend: "Stop on Red Signal". Height: 6·5in (16·51cm).

5 "Easter Bunny Express", made by the Louis Marx company, New York, USA, in 1936. This novelty train in brightly-lithographed tinplate was made only for sale at Easter 1936: the Bunny and its four open wagons, each marked "Bunny Express" and bearing a design of Easter chicks, were marketed as a boxed set complete with an oval of tinplate track (note the flanged wheels). The wagons, it may be noted, are of a suitable shape to

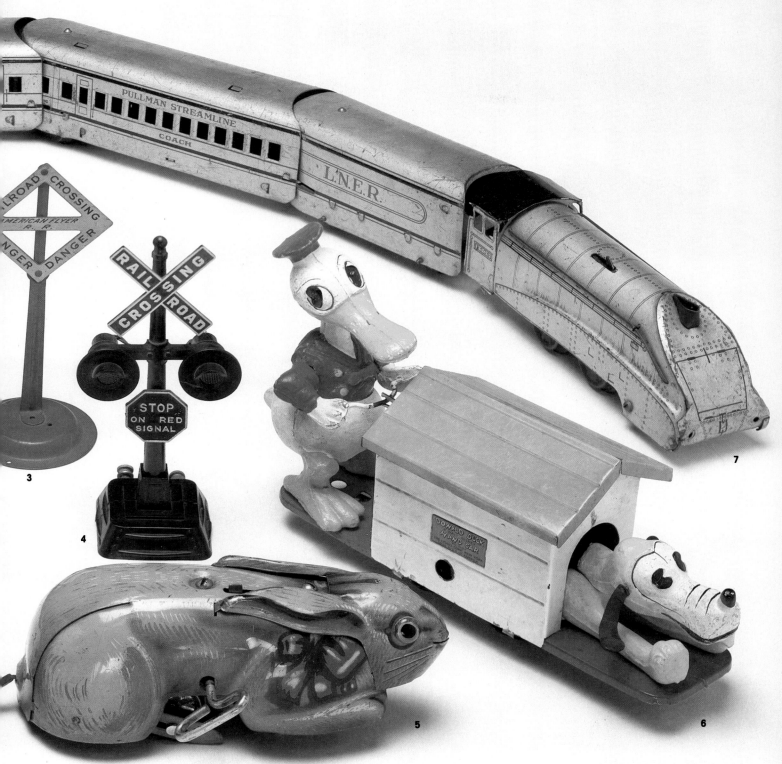

3

4

7

5

6

carry a freight of chocolate eggs! The Bunny itself is clockwork-driven, with a fixed key protruding from its side. The example shown is a complete set—and is believed to be the only complete specimen yet located. It will be appreciated, therefore, that the "Bunny Express" is an extremely rare item and very desirable. The Marx company, founded in 1920, had become one of the largest toy companies in the world by the 1930s, when a British subsidiary was also in production; see (7). Marx is especially known to collectors for tinplate novelty toys and clockwork trains of the cheaper kind. Overall length of "Bunny Express": 30in (76·2cm).

6 Gauge "0" "Donald Duck Hand Car", made by Lionel, in association with the Walt Disney

organization, in 1936-37: the red label above the winding aperture on the kennel side proclaims: "Donald Duck Hand Car/Walt Disney (copyright mark)/Lionel Corporation of America". This amusing clockwork-driven novelty toy in tinplate, showing Pluto pointing the way from his kennel while Donald Duck steers the car, may seem to represent a rather curious departure for a "serious" model railway maker like Lionel; however, such is the appeal of Walt Disney's characters— which have continued to feature in popular toys up to the present day—that the success of this item was most welcome to Lionel at a time when the sales of conventional toy trains were sagging. The car has flanged

wheels and was marketed complete with a circle of Gauge "0" tinplate track. This toy is quite rare and is much desired by collectors, particularly in the United States. Length: 11in (27·94cm).

7 Gauge "0" "Silver Jubilee" Clockwork Train Set, made by Marx, Great Britain, and dating from around 1936. This streamlined "LNER" (London and North Eastern Railway) engine with its articulated "Pullman Streamline" "Coach" and "Coach Buffet" was brought out by the British subsidiary of the Marx company of New York, USA, at a time when Sir Nigel Gresley's striking all-silver express locomotive "Silver Link", hauling the all-streamlined train designed to mark the Silver Jubilee

of King George V and Queen Mary in 1935, had captured the public imagination and was very much in the news. The toy train is of the cheaper variety generally associated with this maker and, like Marx's products in the USA, was chiefly marketed through the cheaper chain-stores, but it is nevertheless a rather attractive item and is certainly most evocative of its period. It was produced also in green livery, and in blue livery with the lettering "LMS" (London, Midland & Scottish Railway). It is interesting to note the strong American influence apparent in the design and finish of the Pullman units, which are in a style more reminiscent of the New York Central Railroad than of the LNER! Length overall: 32in (81·28cm).

1-3 Gauge "00" EDP2 Passenger Electric Train Set, London, Midland & Scottish Railway (LMS). The example shown dates from 1951; the set was first catalogued in 1939 but was not in fact issued until after World War II. It represents a really magnificent attempt by Hornby Dublo at true scale modelling. The diecast 4-6-2 locomotive, numbered "6231", is a faithful representation of a "Duchess Class" then in use by the LMS, with a most comprehensive set of Walschaerts valve gear. This example is named "Duchess of Atholl". The six-wheeled tender has a diecast chassis, tinplate upper half, and plastic coal deck. The bogie coaches also represented a great advance for Hornby Dublo, since although

lithographed they have transparent windows and are fitted with side corridors. Although most collectable when boxed in fine condition, these sets are by no means rare. Lengths (engine and tender): 12in (30·48cm); (coach): 9·0625in (23·02cm).
4 Gauge "00" Southern Railway (SR) Brake Van, c1950. Based on a pre-War model, this is rarer than most Hornby Dublo brake vans. The main difference between pre- and post-War examples is that on the later versions a type of half-buckeye automatic coupling was fitted, whereas a strange, flat, horizontal-sprung device coupled pre-War models. Length: 4·3125in (10·95cm).
5 Gauge "00" High Capacity Brick Wagon. In both pre- and early

post-War versions this was lettered "NE", but it is more often found with the British Railways (BR) prefix "E" only. It is easy to find. Length: 5·75in (14·6cm).
6 Gauge "00" Hornby Dublo EDLT20 "Bristol Castle" Locomotive, numbered "7013", and Six-Wheeled Tender, in BR (Western Region) livery. This model was announced at Christmas 1957, the first addition to the range for some time. Unlike other Hornby Dublo tender locomotives, it has an all-diecast tender, joined to the locomotive by a drawbar. Centre-rail current collectors are fitted beneath the tender. With a new electric motor that had to fit into a reduced space, these locomotives were somewhat underpowered, but later "Castles" had an improved

ring-field motor which extended well into the cab. In the main, the "Castles" are easy to find in three-rail or later two-rail versions. Length (engine and tender): 10·25in (26·035cm).
7 Gauge "00" D20 Composite Restaurant Car. Following soon after (6), this may be found in Western Region chocolate-and-cream or standard BR plum-and-cream. It has a quite convincing interior. These vehicles are easy to find. Length: 9·0625in (23·02cm).
8 Gauge "00" D21 Corridor Coach, Brake Second. Lithographed in Western Region colours for "The Bristolian" train sets, this was made to complement (6) and was a re-lithograph of an LMS item—see (3). It is easy to find. Length: 9·0625in (23·02cm).

9 Gauge "00" 0-6-2 Tank Locomotive, numbered "6699", Great Western Railway (GWR), electric; an item of 1950, from boxed set EDG7, in which the wagons at (10) and (18) also featured. It was made in large numbers both pre- and post-War (available also in clockwork in the former case) in all four major liveries. The GWR and SR versions are the rarer, and clockwork versions in any livery are scarce. Length: 5·5in (13·97cm).

10 Gauge "00" D1 Open Wagon, GWR; an early model, made in great quantity and boxed in most Hornby Dublo freight sets. Length: 3·5in (8·89cm).

11 Gauge "00" D1 Meat Van; a post-War version of an SR vehicle produced pre-War and with a short post-War run. Like many SR items,

it is comparatively scarce. Length: 3·5in (8·89cm).

12 Gauge "00" D1 Cattle Truck, GWR; produced both pre- and post-War. In this instance, the LMS version seems hardest to find. Length: 3·5in (8·89cm).

13 Gauge "00" D1 Petrol Tank Wagon, "Power Ethyl". Available in 1939-40 and for a short time post-War, this is one of the rarer Hornby Dublo wagons. Length: 3·5in (8·89cm).

14 Gauge "00" D1 Petrol Tank Wagon, "Esso". Available as (13), this is one of the most attractive and probably one of the rarest of Hornby Dublo wagons. Length: 3·5in (8·89cm).

15 Gauge "00" D1 Goods Brake Van, GWR. This appeared in all major liveries both pre- and post-War, with a later BR version. GWR

versions are quite hard to find. Length: 4·3125in (10·95cm).

16 Gauge "00" D1 Oil Tank Wagon, "Royal Daylight". As shown, with the "Esso" oval, the wagon is common; an earlier version, lithographed "Royal Daylight" only, is much harder to find. Length: 3·5in (8·89cm).

17 Gauge "00" D1 Tank Wagon, "Esso Petroleum Company"; produced in the mid-1960s as one of a variety of "Esso" colour schemes, and fairly common. Length: 3·5in (8·89cm).

18 Gauge "00" D1 Tank Wagon, "Power Petrol". Available from the early 1950s as a replacement for (13), this is fairly easy to find. Length: 3·5in (8·89cm).

19 Gauge "00" D1 Tank Wagon, "Esso"; a common item, available from the mid-1950s. Many of these wagons

had two-rail plastic wheels fitted when two-rail traction was introduced in the early 1960s. Length: 3·5in (8·89cm).

20 Gauge "00" D1 Tank Wagon, "Shell Lubricating Oil"; available from the mid-1950s, and very easy to find. Length: 3·5in (8·89cm).

21 Gauge "00" EDL18 2-6-4 Tank Locomotive, numbered "80054", BR; available from the mid-1950s and still easy to find in both two- and three-rail versions. Length: 7in (17·78cm).

22-23 Gauge "00" D13 Coaches: Suburban First/Third (22), and Suburban Brake/Third (23), both BR. These were brought out to complement (21), and were later re-tooled with transparent windows. They are easy to find. Length: 7·9375in (20·16cm).

In the years following World War II, toy and model railway enthusiasts in the United States of America sought for something better to collect than the mass-produced items, both of domestic origin and imported from abroad, then generally available. Although many of these mass-produced models represented a considerable improvement in accuracy over their pre-World War II counterparts, enthusiasts demanded still greater detail and realism.

In the early 1950s, Max Gray, an American model railway buff, supplied a Japanese watchmaker with super-precision lost wax castings and highly detailed drawings and photographs of locomotives. Working from these materials, the watchmaker produced beautiful locomotive models in brass, initially in Gauge "H0" and later in Gauge "0", detailed down to the last rivet and almost rivalling in quality the finest "one-off" models. These models were mostly produced in fairly small batches, principally by K.T.M., Tenshodo, and some other Japanese firms which were commissioned to undertake such work. They were generally supplied as shown on this spread: unpainted, in a lacquered brass finish. Production continued sporadically in Japan until the late 1960s; some similar models were later made in South Korea — see (7) and (8) — but these were generally inferior to the earlier Japanese products.

Although they cannot, strictly speaking, be described as toys, Japanese brass models are of great interest to collectors and thus fully justify their inclusion in this book.

All the trains shown on this spread were photographed at the London Toy and Model Museum, October House, 21/23 Craven Hill, London W2.

1 Gauge "0" (¼in scale) 4-8-8-4 "Big Boy" Locomotive and Twelve-Wheeled Tender, Union Pacific Railroad, made by K.T.M., Japan, and dating from 1967. This is a Japanese brass model of very high quality, fully-detailed down to the rivets, with all fittings, and with no fewer than 38 sprung wheels. Its powerful electric motors make it capable of hauling a scale train (see below). This example is the property of the author, currently on loan to the London Toy and Model Museum, and was acquired in 1967 as a new item by trading a Bassett-Lowke train with an American collector. It is modelled on the "U.P. 4000" Class, the world's largest steam locomotives ever to go into production, built by the American Locomotive Company for the Union Pacific Railroad in 1941-42. These locomotives were designed to eliminate the need for double-heading on the heavy freight trains of the "Overland Route", which involved long climbs that included crossing the summit of Mount Sherman; they were also used to haul huge troop trains during World War II. The ultimate single-expansion articulated locomotive, "Big Boy"

could develop 7,000hp and could head a freight train of 70 cars, weighing 4,000 tons (4,064 tonnes), at speeds of up to 70mph (113 km/h). Length (engine and tender): 35in (88·9cm).

2 Gauge "0" 4-8-2 Locomotive and Twelve-Wheeled Tender, made for Max Gray by K.T.M., Japan, and dating from around 1960. The model is in a bright-lacquered finish. See also (3) and (4). Length (engine and tender): 27in (68·58cm).

3 Gauge "0" M1.A 4-8-2 Locomotive and Twelve-Wheeled Tender, Pennsylvania Railroad, by K.T.M., Japan. Although this locomotive is somewhat duller in appearance than the other examples of Japanese brass shown on this spread, closer inspection will reveal that it is even more highly detailed than

is usual with such models. This probably indicates that it is an early example, made for Max Gray and dating from the 1950s. Length (engine and tender): 25·875in (65·725cm).

4 Gauge "0" J3A Streamlined 4-6-4 Hudson Locomotive and Twelve-Wheeled Tender, New York Central Railroad; a marvellous model made for Max Gray by K.T.M. and dating from around 1960. Note the breath-taking front end of the locomotive, so aptly described by Edwin Alexander as reminiscent of an ancient warrior's helmet. The prototype was designed in 1937 by Henry Dreyfuss, and the locomotives of this class were used on fast trains; notably hauling the famous "20th Century Limited" which made the New York-Chicago run in 16

hours. Beautifully finished and finely detailed, this Japanese brass model shows the locomotive looking exactly as it did when heading the "Limited"! Length (engine and tender): 26in (66cm).

5 Gauge "H0" (Narrow Gauge) 2-8-0 Freight Locomotive and Eight-Wheeled Tender; this rather attractive little model was made by Westside, Japan, and dates from around 1965. Length (engine and tender): 13·5in (34·29cm).

6 Gauge "H0" Railbus, modelled on a South American prototype. This diminutive model of an interesting vehicle was probably made by K.T.M., Japan, and dates from around 1965. Length: 3·75in (9·525cm).

7 Gauge "H0" 2-6-2 Prairie Tank Locomotive of the Great Western

Railway (GWR). This model of a once-familiar type of British locomotive, like the similar item shown at (8), was produced for the British market by an unidentified South Korean maker. Dating from around 1970, it is of a later date than the other brass models shown on this spread and, as may be seen, displays considerably less detail than its Japanese-made predecessors. Length: 5·25in (13·335cm).

8 Gauge "H0" 0-6-0 Pannier Tank Locomotive; another model based on a once-familiar Great Western Railway (GWR) type and produced for the British market by an unidentified South Korean maker; see (7) for further remarks on these later brass models. Length: 4·25in (10·795cm).

The Aster Cash Register Company of Tokyo, Japan, began to produce model locomotives in the mid-1970s, entering the field, it seems, simply because its owner happened to be a model railway enthusiast. It remains in production in this field today as the Aster Hobby Company Inc., Tokyo. Although some of its models have been made only in limited numbers, many of the earlier examples are still obtainable. New items are constantly aded to the range, the most recent at the time of writing being an excellent three-cylinder representation of the Gresley-designed "A4 Class" Pacific "Mallard" of the London and North Eastern Railway (LNER), the locomotive which, in 1938, in real life established a world steam speed

record of 126mph (203km/h). Aster locomotives can be purchased at good model shops, but are by no means cheap. They may best be described as expensive toys for adults, appealing particularly to collectors who enjoy running as well as displaying their trains—and they are certainly collectable items of the future. Aster models are marketed in Europe through Fulgurex of Lausanne, Switzerland (headed by the famous collector Count Antonio Giansanti-Coluzzi) and in the United States of America through Gauge "1" America of Danville, Pa..
Constructed throughout of steel and brass, Aster locomotives may be obtained either ready-to-run or in kit form. They normally feature

twin cylinders, spirit-fired Smithies-type boiler, slip-eccentric reversing, and a full range of cab fittings. Some—like (1) and (4) below—have a manual water-pump fitted in the tender. They normally work at high pressure: around 50 psi, as compared to around 15 psi for a conventional steam-powered model locomotive.

1 Gauge "1" 0-4-0 Locomotive, "Reno", and Eight-Wheeled Tender (two bogies): a model of the type of wood-burning locomotive familiar to all devotees of the "Wild West"—and not unlike the famous "General" of the Buster Keaton movie—with its big smokestack and cowcatcher (or "pilot", as the latter is more correctly called). It is modelled

on the locomotives built in the 1870s by the noted Baldwin works for the Virginia and Truckee Railroad, and is finished in that railway's colours. Length (engine and tender, including cowcatcher): 23·5in (59·69cm).
2 Gauge "1" 4-4-0 Locomotive, "Winchester", and Six-Wheeled Tender, numbered "901", in Southern Railway livery; note also the Aster trademark on the side of the cab. The prototype dated from the late 1920s, when Britain's Southern Railway needed a new four-coupled locomotive for its Hastings line, an awkward route with sharp curves and restricted tunnels. The requirement was met by the "V Class", a three-cylinder locomotive with large driving wheels, which became the most

powerful 4-4-0 in Europe. Some 40 "V Class" locomotives were built in 1930-35 and, since most were named after wellknown boys' schools in the Southern Railway's area of operations, they were known as the "Schools Class". The example shown here is particularly interesting in that it was the very first model off the Aster production line: it was sent to Britain for evaluation in 1975, and has since run many thousands of scale miles on the author's layout. At the time of writing (December 1984) it is undergoing its first major overhaul. Length (engine and tender): 22in (55·88cm).

3Gauge "1" 0-6-0 Tank Engine, numbered "335", in the livery of the Great Eastern Railway (GER). This locomotive is the odd one out on this spread, since it works at low pressure, having a single oscillating cylinder between the frames. It was originally produced by Aster as model of a locomotive built by Fives-Lille for the Western Railway of France in the late 1880s. At the turn of the century, Messrs Holden was commissioned by the GER to build very similar locomotives for the British railway. Although it is, therefore, not completely true-to-prototype, this is a most attractive model, with ultramarine livery and correct lettering. Length: 11·5in (29·21cm).

4Gauge "1" Shay Geared Class B Locomotive, numbered "6": an intriguing representation of the logging locomotive designed by Ephraim Shay in the 1860s, during the American Civil War, when there was a much increased all-the-year-round demand for timber. Unlike conventional locomotives, the Shays had powered bogies (which are beautifully reproduced in the model) to enable them to negotiate steep grades, rough track, and sharp curves. They moved at very slow speeds, hardly more than walking pace. The wheel arrangement is correctly described as "BB" (0-4-0 + 0-4-0). By the 1920s, Shay locomotives were still by far the most popular form of haulage in the logging industry, and there are still one or two that remain at work today in the forests of the Far East. Length: 17in (43·18cm).

5Gauge "1" 2-6-0 Mogul Locomotive, numbered "8550", and Six-Wheeled (one axle; one bogie) Tender. This attractive little locomotive is based on a prototype made around the turn of the century by the American Locomotive Company's Schenectady works for the Kyushu Railway Company of Japan. It is interesting to note that a substantial number of these locomotives were supplied to the Midland Railway of Britain, which was suffering from a shortage of locomotives at that time. Presumably to allow it to be sold at a lower price, this model of the locomotive is fitted with one working cylinder only, the other being a dummy. Nevertheless, it has performed very well on the author's layout. and looks particularly attractive when hauling a light freight train. Length (engine and tender): 20·5in (52·07cm).

With the exception of (1), the property of the author, all the trains shown on this spread were photographed by courtesy of Hadley Hobbies, London.

1 Gauge "1" "A4 Class" Pacific Locomotive, "Mallard", numbered "4468", and Eight-Wheeled Tender, in London and North Eastern Railway (LNER) livery, by Aster, Japan. Appearing in 1984, this magnificent model of Sir Nigel Gresley's famous streamlined "Mallard", which in 1938 set a world record for steam traction with a speed of 126mph (203km/h), is the latest addition to the Aster company's range of Gauge "1" steam locomotives, shown on *pages 116-117*. Built to a scale of 1:32in, this model is fitted, like its prototype,

with three cylinders (two outside; one inside). The fire-tube copper boiler is spirit-fired and is fitted with two safety-valves, regulator, blower, check-valve, and pressure and water gauges. All the wheels are of stainless steel with coil springs. The tender, carrying water and spirit, is fitted with a hand-operated water pump. Length (engine and tender): 27·2in (69·1cm).

2 Gauge "H0" 2-8-2 Freight Locomotive and Eight-Wheeled Tender, German Federal Railways, by Gebrüder Märklin, West Germany; an electric-driven model, currently available. It is modelled on a German "Class 41" locomotive: these were first built in 1936 and some 366 entered service. The model, constructed of diecast zinc and plastic, is a faithful represen-

tation of the prototype and is well up to Märklin's high standard: all ten driving wheels are powered and it is fitted with working headlights, a smoke unit, and simulated Heusinger valve gear. Length (engine and tender): 10·83in (27·5cm).

3 Gauge "00" Streamlined "A4 Class" Pacific Locomotive, "Sir Nigel Gresley", numbered "4482", and Eight-Wheeled Tender, in LNER green livery; electric, issued by Hornby, Great Britain, in around 1965. Length (engine and tender): 11·25in (28·575cm).

4 Gauge "H0" Diesel Locomotive; an electric-driven model by Märklin-Hamo, West Germany, dating from around 1965. This diecast zinc model, with working headlights, is based on the "V160 Class" BB Locomotives built for general

purpose use on the German Federal Railways. Length: 8·27in (21cm).

5 Gauge "00" 4-6-2 "City of Carlisle" Locomotive, in maroon livery with British Railway's numbering "46238", and Six-Wheeled Tender; electric, by Wren, Great Britain, and currently available. The model is based on the last Pacifics designed for the London, Midland & Scottish Railway (LMS) by Sir William Stanier in 1947. Length (engine and tender): 12in (30·48cm).

6 Gauge "00" "6P Class" 4-6-0 Locomotive, "Grenadier Guardsman", numbered "46110", and Six-Wheeled Tender, by Wren. This electric-driven model, in British Railways (BR) green livery, is currently available. Length (engine and tender): 10·25in (26·035cm).

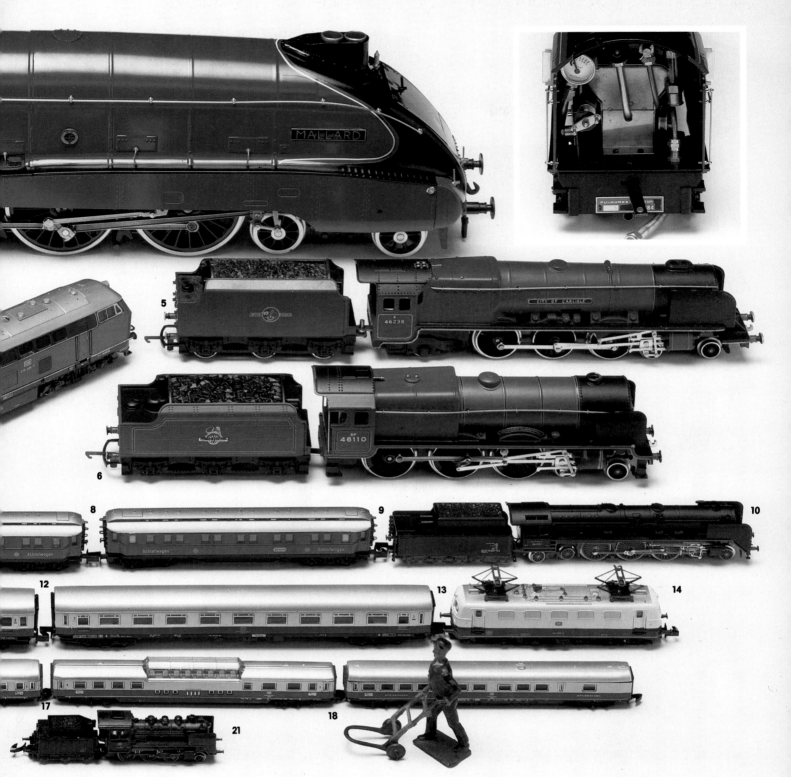

7 Gauge "H0" 2-6-0 (Mogul) Locomotive and Six-Wheeled Tender, by Fleischmann, West Germany, dating from around 1970. This model of a "Class 24" locomotive of German Federal Railways has a diecast body and working headlights. Length (engine and tender): 8·66in (22cm).

8-10 Gauge "N" 4-6-4 Locomotive and Ten-Wheeled Tender (10), and two Sleeping Cars (8-9), German Federal Railways; an electric-driven model, currently available, by Arnold, West Germany. The diecast model locomotive is well detailed and is fitted with a smoke unit. It runs on 9mm Gauge "N" track: Arnold pioneered Gauge "N" railways in 1960. The sleeping cars of vintage type are modelled on prototypes that ran on the Royal

Prussian Railway. Lengths (locomotive and tender): 6·46in (16·4cm); (coach): 4·92in (12·5cm).

11-14 Gauge "N" Type BR141 BO-BO Electric Multi-Purpose Locomotive (14), with First Class Coach (13), Second Class Coach (12), and Baggage Car (11); another Gauge "N" electric train, currently available, by Arnold, West Germany. The three scale-length express coaches have electric lighting. Lengths (locomotive): 3·74in (9·5cm); (coach): 6·5in (16·5cm).

15-18 Gauge "Z" Märklin Mini-Club 2-8-2 Locomotive and Eight-Wheeled Tender (15), with three Tee coaches (Tee coaches, the pride of German Federal Railways, are all First Class): Compartment Car (16), Dome Observation Car (17), and Dining Car (18). This

electric train is a current item offered by Märklin in Gauge "Z", to a scale of 1:220mm and running on 6·5mm track, a system invented by Märklin in 1972 and exclusive to this maker. It is the smallest model railway commercially available and items are fairly expensive, which is hardly surprising when one considers the near-watchmaking precision required in the construction of the tiny locomotives, many of which are complete with full valve-gear. The locomotive shown here is a Gauge "Z" version of the "H0" model at (2). Lengths (locomotive and tender): 4·41in (11·2cm); (coach): 4·72in (12cm).

19-20 Gauge "Z" Märklin Mini-Club Baggage Cars, German Federal Railways, Type DM902; another mini-gauge item currently available

from Märklin. Length (each coach): 4·72in (12cm).

21 Gauge "Z" Märklin Mini-Club 2-6-0 Locomotive and Six-Wheeled Tender. This electric-driven model of a "Class 24" passenger locomotive of German Federal Railways is another of the mini-gauge items currently available. Length (engine and tender): 3·23in (8·2cm).

Inset Closeup view of the cab of "Mallard" (1) shows the many fittings: pressure gauge, regulator valve, blower valve, check valve, and water gauge. The flexible hose is the connection for water supply from the tender. The maker's plate shows that this model was marketed through Fulgurex of Switzerland, and that it is number 006 of a limited batch dated 1984.

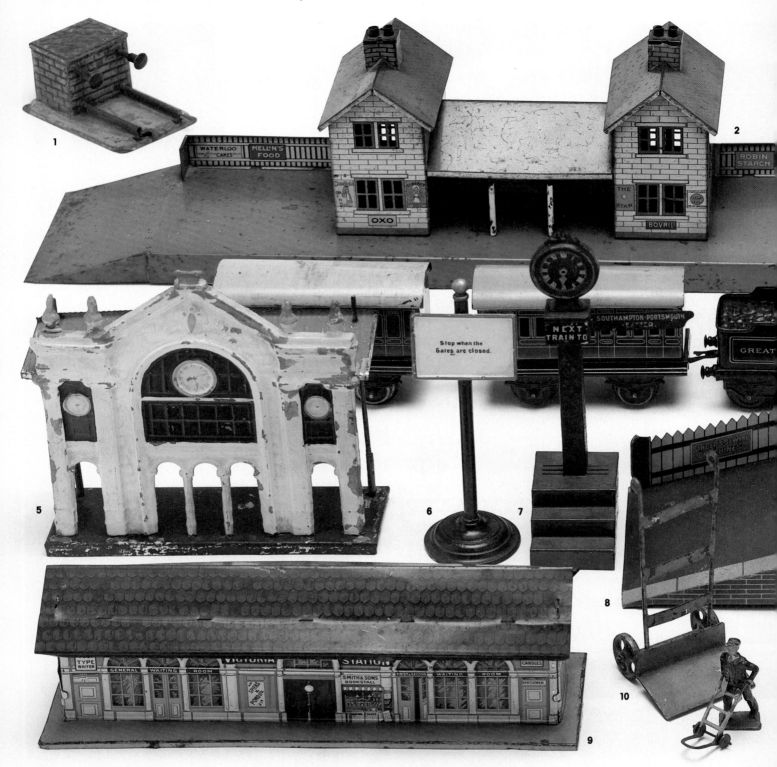

1 Gauge "0" Buffers, tinplate, made by Gebrüder Bing, Nuremburg, Germany. This hand-painted accessory dates from around 1906, when it was catalogued by A.W. Gamage, London, at a price of 1s 3d (6p, 7c) in Gauge "0", 1s 6d (7½p, 9c) in Gauge "1", and 1s 9d (8½p, 10c) in Gauge "2". A Bing trademark is stamped between the rails. Length of base: 4·5in (11·43cm).

2 Station, tinplate, for use with Gauge "0" trains, made by Bing and first catalogued by Gamage's in 1913, when it was described as "a realistic model English railway station, in fine polychrome japanning with advertisements in correct colours . . . 22 inches (55·88cm) long . . . 3s 11d (19½p, 23c)." A larger

version, 26in (66·04cm) long, was also available at a price of 5s 11d (29½p, 35c). This model remained in Gamage's Catalogue well into the 1920s, and was listed in Bing's own English-language Catalogue as late as 1928, by which time the price of the version shown here had risen to 6s 9d (33½p, 40c). The front of the station is shown here; the rear is equally well-detailed. It is, indeed a most attractive specimen, made even more interesting and desirable by the wealth of contemporary advertising signs, a feature much appreciated by all toy collectors. The base is pierced to allow the insertion of lighted candles to illuminate the buildings, with an added touch of realism then provided

with smoke from the chimneys.

3 Train Indicator, tinplate, by an unidentified German maker and dating from about 1910. The accessory is in continental style, but this example, showing British towns as destinations, was obviously made for the UK market —although no railway normally served stations so widely separated as Glasgow, Blackpool, Liverpool, Southport, Birmingham, and Brighton! The same model, with appropriate destinations, was produced for the European market. Base: 4·5in x 2·75in (11·43cm x 6·98cm); maximum height: 8in (20·32cm).

4 Gauge "0" Tunnel by an unidentified German maker; an early railway accessory dating from around 1900. It is of tinplate

and is constructed in two halves for easier packaging, and is attractively hand-painted with landscape details. Length: 8·5in (21·59cm); width: 5in (12·7cm); maximum height: 8·5in (21·59cm). The train seen approaching the tunnel is a Gauge "0" 0-4-0 "Vulcan" Great Western Railway locomotive and tender, with two passenger coaches, made by Bing in the mid-1920s.

5 Station for Gauge "0" trains, by an unidentified German maker and dating from around 1900, or possibly earlier. This very simple accessory of hand-painted tinplate is no more than a station façade on a base; nevertheless, it has a certain elegance and is a desirable item. Length of base: 7·25in

(18·41cm); maximum height: 7·25in (18·41cm).

6 Railway Sign, "Stop when the Gates are closed"; a simple lineside accessory in handpainted tinplate by Bing, Germany, dating from around 1900. Height: 7in (17·78cm).

7 Clock and Indicator, tinplate on a tinplate stand, by an unidentified German maker and dating from around 1900. Since the destination board shows "Southampton-Portsmouth-Exeter", this example was obviously intended for the British market; as with (3), the same model would have been produced with appropriate destinations for sale on the continent. Like a number of other accessories on this spread, it is in no particular scale and is intended for use with toy railways of any gauge. Height: 7·75in (19·68cm).

8 Wayside Station by Bing; a most pleasingly lithographed tinplate item, again with interesting advertisements of the period, including the ubiquitous "Oxo" and "Bovril" along with other present-day survivors such as "Lux" (soap) and "Wright's Coal Tar Soap" —as well as the now-vanished "Zebra the Blacklead" (for cleaning fire-grates). It is nicely proportioned and the station building, as shown here, has an opening door. This accessory was listed in Bing's English-language Catalogue for 1928 at a price of 4s 9d (23½p, 28c). Length overall: 19·5in (49·53cm); maximum height: 7·5in (19·05cm).

9 "Victoria Station" by Bing; a small but colourfully lithographed tinplate model—somewhat incongruously named, since Victoria is a major London terminus—listed in Gamage's 1906 Catalogue, as a "Local Railway Station", at a price of 0s 9d (3½p, 4c). The lithographed detail is identical on both sides; again, there are a number of interesting advertisements. Note particularly the "Smith & Sons Bookstall"—the bookstalls of W.H. Smith are still a prominent feature on many British stations —and the "Gentlemen" (lavatory) to the right. This model like (2), could be illuminated with candles. Length of base: 10·75in (27·3cm); width: 3·25in (8·25cm); height: 3·5in (8·89cm).

10 Porter's Hand Barrow, a tinplate accessory, probably of German manufacture, listed in Gamage's 1902 Catalogue at a price of 1s 0d (5p, 6c). It is immediately obvious that this large model is completely out of scale with any toy train. Length overall: 5·25in (13·33cm).

11-20 Figures and Station Furniture, dating approximately between 1910 and 1935. The Bench and Passenger at (11) and (12), the Nurse (16), Lady in Edwardian Dress (17), Passenger (18), Lady in 1920s Dress (19), and Clergyman (20), are all hollow-cast figures made by Britains, Great Britain. The Platform Machine (13), Weighing Machine (14), and Chocolate Vending Machine (15), are by unidentified makers.

121

1 Transformer Unit by Jep, France, dating from the 1920s-30s. This quaint hut is an excellent method of disguising an essential but utilitarian component of an electric train set. Some other makers produced similar items, and it is surprising that the idea was not more widely adopted. Items of this kind are very collectable and are quite hard to find.

2 Oil Lamp Standard by Bing, Germany c1905. This delightful model has a paraffin reservoir in a tube concealed down its length and a wick in its ventilated glass lantern. Like many of the accessories shown on this spread, it is in no particular scale. Collectors place a high value on these oil lamps; they are hard to acquire, since their appeal is not limited to railway enthusiasts.

3 Electric Lamp Standard by Bing, 1920s. This small lamp is one of many varieties of electric lamp produced by both Bing and Märklin. Another very desirable collector's item of wide appeal.

4 Train Indicator and Clock Pedestal by Bing, made for the British market (note lettering of boards) in the late 1920s. Bing produced many items of station furniture of this kind. This would be in place only on a platform of huge scale—but is probable that play-value was the maker's primary consideration.

5 Train Route Indicator, in continental style, by Märklin, Germany, dating from c1930. Hand-painted and with rubber-stamped lettering, this is one of Märklin's many delightful, high-quality accessories and, like many similar items that were perhaps not so highly valued in their time, it is rare.

6 Gauge "0" Distant Bracket Signal by Bassett-Lowke, Great Britain; an accessory made both before and after World War II. These Northampton-made signals have a nearer-scale appearance than their Hornby counterparts, and although not highly prized, they certainly would look better on a vintage layout.

7 Indication Post by Märklin, 1930s; a rather unusual-looking item of continental-style track furniture. Like all Märklin items, it is collectable, although not highly desirable.

8 Gauge "0" No 2 Signal Cabin by Hornby, Great Britain; made both before and after World War II. The roof opens to give access to the lever frame, see (13). There was also a cheaper No 1 version. These are among the most common Hornby buildings.

9 Gauge "0" Junction Sign by Jep, mid-1930s; an electrically-lit accessory in French style. Not particularly valuable, but of interest to Jep collectors.

10 Luggage Weighing Post by Kibri, Germany, 1930s. Again, an accessory in which play-value is the primary consideration, with working scales. Kibri's range of buildings and accessories does not occupy a high place in the attention of most collectors.

11 Gauge "00" "Table-Top" Signal Box by Bing: one of the attractive

little buildings produced in the 1920s to complement the maker's compact Gauge "00" systems in electric and clockwork. This equipment has recently increased in collecting popularity.

12 Gauge "00" "Table-Top" Level Crossing by Bing, c 1927. This is for the clockwork system: electric items are more difficult to find.

13 Gauge "0" Lever Frame by Hornby, made from the mid-1920s until World War II. This well-made accessory could operate from a signal cabin—see (13)—to control trains on the track. These items, with black or blue bases, are eagerly sought and are scarce.

14 Gauge "1" Hydraulic Buffers by Bing, mid-1920s. This Gauge "1" version is quite rare, although Gauge "0" hydraulic buffers by

Bing, Hornby, and Bassett-Lowke are among the more easily-found "unusual" accessories.

15-16 Gauge "0" Railway Accessories No 8: Notice Boards, by Hornby; items from a boxed set of six pieces, available from the late 1920s until World War II. As boxed sets, these Hornby items are rare and most desirable.

17 Gauge "1" Gateman's Hut; this pre-1914 item may be by Carette, Germany, although it shows strong Märklin influence. Although charming, it is not of great collectable importance. Nor is the item shown immediately below it: a Gauge "0" Platform Water Crane by Exley, Great Britain, first catalogued in the mid-1930s. Made of brass, this is a simple model of high quality.

18 Gauge "0" Railway Accessories No 7: Workman's Hut, Brazier, Shovel and Poker, by Hornby; a delightful accessory, not often found complete, made from c 1930 until World War II.

19 Gauge "0" Railway Accessories No 2: Gradient Posts and Mile Posts; a Hornby accessory made from 1929 until World War II. A boxed set is hard to find.

20 Gauge "0" Platform Accessories No 1: Miniature Luggage; made by Hornby until World War II. Complete with porter's barrow, this is a most collectable set, and not particularly rare.

21 Hall's Distemper Advertisement, Dinky Toys No 13, made by Meccano for its Gauge "0" Hornby layouts. This is a highly-prized lineside accessory, consisting of two lead

figures with a cardboard sign, and is exceptionally hard to find in complete condition.

22 Gauge "0" "Table-Top" Passenger Station, Bing, 1927. One of the larger "Table-Top" items, this is made in three pieces, with side clips to hold it at the right distance from the track. A "must" for Bing collectors; not very scarce.

23 Gauge "00" Table-Top" Locomotive Shed, Bing, mid-to-late 1920s. Made in both electric and clockwork versions (the latter shown here), it is one of the rarer "Table-Top" items.

24 Gauge "0" M Wayside Station, available from Hornby throughout the 1930s, and made to complement the maker's cheap "M Series" train sets. This is easy to find.

Most commercially-produced items that are now collected originally were listed in their maker's catalogues—and often these are the most important sources of information, and the hardest to find. The examples seen here represent only a fraction of the extant material. Some rarer catalogues, like those of Märklin—see (7) and (8)—and the "Hornby Book of Trains" series—see (3) and (4)—are now very expensive, but some specialist publishers have now produced compilations of material from old catalogues.

1 "Model Railways 1¼in and 1¾in Gauge" (ie, Gauges "0" and "1"), produced by Bassett-Lowke, Great Britain, in 1912. Bassett-Lowke

catalogues are especially interesting in that they list trains by the famous German makers Bing and Carette, along with some British-made items. A comprehensive collection of pre-World War I Bassett-Lowke catalogues would be invaluable to any collector—but would be very costly to assemble.

2 Shop Advertising of the 1930s: one of the delightful display signs of stiff card—this one showing a Hornby No 2 Special "Yorkshire" clockwork train of c1934—issued by Meccano of Liverpool. This kind of ephemeral material is very hard to find.

3 "Hornby Book of Trains" for 1939-1940: perhaps the most interesting of the series in that it is the only one to list the

Hornby Dublo items, including the "Duchess of Atholl" model so dramatically illustrated on the cover, that were designed pre-War but did not enter production until after 1945.

4 "Hornby Book of Trains" for 1927-1928; opened to show an interesting selection of the items then available, including the Metropolitan Train Set (top left) and the famous "Riviera Blue Train". The little No 1 0-4-0 locomotive is shown in some of its many colour schemes.

5 Hornby Dublo Catalogue of Electric Trains, c1959: a fold-out brochure dating from the period when Hornby Dublo was listing both 3-rail and the new 2-rail systems, and was venturing into both diesel-

outline models and plastic construction methods.

6 Hornby Dublo: another fold-out catalogue, dating from c1957, and proudly displaying the firm's new "Castle Class" locomotive.

7 Märklin Catalogue of c1934. This German-language catalogue from the famous Göppingen firm lists a wealth of Märklin's late series Gauge "0" items, plus a range of Gauge "1" locomotives and equipment. The back end is devoted to Märklin's non-railway products, including model workshop power tools, stationary steam plant, and a fine series of military vehicles and guns, even including toy pistols and revolvers, as well as many non-military toys.

8 Märklin Catalogue of c1939-40. This colour publication lists a

magnificent range of Gauge "0" locomotives then being produced for the home market, including a range of superb electric-outline Swiss locomotives, the French "Mountain Class", and the famous "Borsig Stromlinien-lokomotive" of German Railways. Gauge "1" has now disappeared from the catalogue, and Gauge "00" has made its appearance. As at (7), non-railway items are listed towards the end.

9 Catalogue issued by Mills Brothers of Sheffield (Milbro) in the mid-1930s: a black-and-white publication listing the very expensive models, almost entirely hand-made, then available. The first illustration is of a Gauge "0" LNER locomotive, numbered "10000", in high

pressure steam, priced at £17 17s 0d (£17.85, $21.42). The company would make almost any railway item to order, but it is probably best known to collectors for its fine range of coaches, especially those in LNER teak finish.

10 "Lionel Electric Trains": a catalogue of the 1930s produced by The Lionel Corporation, New York, for the British market and depicting, among other items seen, Lionel's famous diesel-outline express based on "City of Portland". It also includes items made by Lionel in the larger "Standard Gauge".

11 "Model Railways": a Bassett-Lowke catalogue of c1927, in black-and-white, illustrating mainly Bing-type locomotives and vehicles in Gauges "0" and "1".

12 "Bassett-Lowke Gauge "0" Scale Model Railways", c1949. A much smaller variety of stock is listed than in (11), but certain pre-War favourites still appear, along with the firm's ever-popular standard steam locomotives.

13 "Bassett-Lowke Model Railways Gauge "0"", Spring 1953. Most items are shown in British Railways livery, and newcomers include a handsome taper-boiler version of "Royal Scot".

14 Catalogue of Gauge "00" Scenery and Effects, issued by Hamblings, Great Britain, 1950s. This firm made many interesting items for Gauge "00" layouts; notably, lithographed sheet-card cutouts that made up into delightful models of typical English village buildings.

15 "Trix Twin Railway": a fold-out catalogue of the mid-1950s, listing Gauge "00" items. Trix trains were made in Britain by Precision Models, part of the Bassett-Lowke organization.

16 Catalogue issued by Fournereau, France, c1950. This maker, especially noted for beautiful and highly-priced models of French locomotives, took over the Marescot company of France in the 1930s.

17 "Meccano": a general catalogue issued in 1953. Hornby Dublo takes pride of place among the railway items. Hornby Gauge "0" was by now a travesty of its pre-War glory, and no locomotives larger than the mid-series 0-4-0, no bogie vehicles and no electric items are listed.

Index